AMERICA
IN THE
20TH
CENTURY

1980-1989

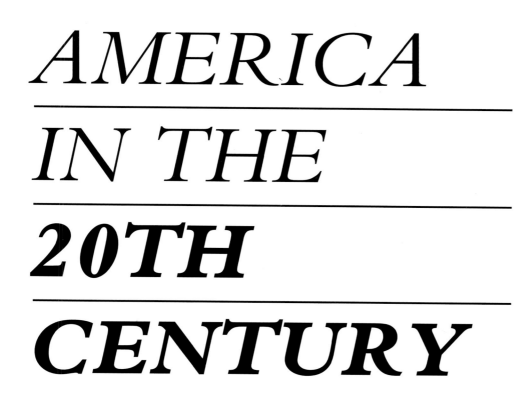

AMERICA IN THE 20TH CENTURY

SECOND EDITION
Revised and Expanded with Primary Sources

1980-1989

David Wright

MARSHALL CAVENDISH
NEW YORK • LONDON • TORONTO • SYDNEY

Marshall Cavendish
99 White Plains Road
Tarrytown, NY 10591

Website: www.marshallcavendish.com

Library of Congress Cataloging-in-Publication Data

America in the 20th Century.-- 2nd ed., rev. and expanded with primary sources.
    p. cm.
Includes bibliographical references and index.
ISBN 0-7614-7364-5 (set)
    1. United States -- Civilization -- 20th century. I. Title: America in the twentieth century.
E169.1.A471872   2003
973.9--dc21
                                            2001052949
    ISBN 0-7614-7373-4 (vol. 9)

Printed in Malaysia
Bound in the United States of America

06 05 04 03 02   5 4 3 2 1

Series created by Discovery Books

Series Editor: Paul Humphrey
Academic Consultants: Gregory Bush,
Chair of History Department, University of Miami, Coral Gables
Richard J. Taylor, History Department, University of Wisconsin, Parkside
Marshall Cavendish Editor: Peter Mavrikis
Marshall Cavendish Production Manager: Alan Tsai
Project Editors: Valerie Weber and Helen Dwyer
Picture Research: Gillian Humphrey
Design Concept: Laurie Shock
Designers: Ian Winton and Winsome Malcolm

*(Frontispiece) President Ronald Reagan and Soviet General Secretary Mikhail Gorbachev in
Moscow's Red Square in May 1988.*

Contents

CHAPTER 1
Assessing the Seventies, Experiencing the Eighties

> *"Our optimism [must be] turned loose again .... People who talk about an age of limits are really talking about their own limitations, not America's."*
>
> Ronald Reagan

Sometimes, the truth hurts. The truth mortally wounded President Jimmy Carter in 1979, when he told Americans in his most famous speech that the country lacked resolve — that it suffered from a "crisis of confidence." Already unpopular, Carter became one of the most-disliked chief executives of the century. Most Americans wanted pep talks, not handwringing, from their president. The faults Jimmy Carter saw in 1970s America were seen by citizens as somehow his fault. They were many and varied.

The 1970s began with Richard M. Nixon running the country and with Spiro T. Agnew as his vice president. Nixon weathered the Vietnam War in part by joining advisor Henry Kissinger in lying about or concealing illegal military actions that killed thousands of people in Southeast Asia. The president got away with deceit abroad, but illegal acts eventually caught up with him at home. Vice President Agnew had taken bribe money while governor of Maryland and all but admitted it by pleading no contest to the criminal charge of failing to pay taxes on the bribe. He resigned in disgrace in 1973 and was replaced by Gerald Ford of Michigan, the leading Republican in the U.S. House of Representatives.

Nixon and his advisors weren't always connected to reality. George McGovern, nominated by left-leaning Democrats, didn't have a prayer of winning the 1972 presidential election. But nevertheless Nixon backers ordered a break-in of Democratic party headquarters in Washington's Watergate apartment complex for a look around. The crooks were caught, and the trail of knowledge about this "third-rate burglary" ended at the White House. Seeing his cronies admit to their crimes and faced with endless embarrassment and certain impeachment, Nixon resigned in 1974. He was automatically succeeded by Gerald Ford.

Ford — and Carter two years after him — could hardly have taken the helm at a worse time. The country, admittedly or not, had just lost a war. The postwar economy was a combination of stagnation and inflation that the experts labeled "stagflation." Prices rose steeply, and there was no economic growth. Interest rates on home mortgages and loans for cars and home improvements headed toward the 20 percent mark — an increase of 300 percent or more in less than a decade. Though interest rates on investments often exceeded 15 percent, the dollar bought less and less every day for months at a time. Economists and ordinary citizens alike feared the kind of nightmarish inflation seen in Germany after World War I, where a wheelbarrow filled with money would buy no more than a loaf of bread.

Initially, voters turned their wrath on Gerald Ford, but only in part

President Carter at the 1980 Democratic National Convention. He sought reelection at a time when America was suffering from high inflation and unemployment, low economic growth, and an energy crisis brought on by rising oil prices. On top of these problems, the Iranian hostage crisis was still unresolved, making America appear weak and indecisive.

because of the sour economy. Ford had quickly issued a pardon to Richard Nixon, despite the fact that most of the country wanted to try — and convict — the former president. Jimmy Carter, the governor of Georgia, ran successfully against Ford by emphasizing that he was a Washington outsider. He and running mate Walter Mondale, a U.S. senator from Minnesota, outpolled Ford and Senator Robert Dole of Kansas by 1.8 million votes. Carter's four years were similar to Ford's two: Jobs, productivity, economic growth, and most other matters to which Americans attach importance failed to show positive movement. The so-called misery

"This is the most serious threat to world peace during my administration. It's even more serious than Hungary or Czechoslovakia."

Jimmy Carter, on the Soviet invasion of Afghanistan

index, which is a combination of inflation and unemployment figures, showed Jimmy Carter's term to be the most difficult for the American people since World War II.

Annoying Everyone

President Carter announced on January 4, 1980, that the U.S. would punish the Soviet Union for its invasion of Afghanistan by stopping exports of grain and high-technology equipment to the huge nation. This angered farmers and shippers and resulted in more surplus grain than usual being stored under plastic covers in fields and along roads and railroad sidings. At Carter's request, the U.S. Olympic Committee voted on April 12, 1980, not to attend the Moscow Summer Games. The action upset athletes, fans, television executives, and those who had planned to attend the games. Group by group, Carter seemed to be alienating everyone.

A worry that surfaced long before Jimmy Carter, one which intensified throughout the 1980s, was the federal deficit. Not since 1964 had Washington been able to balance its huge

Jimmy Carter.

James Earl (Jimmy) Carter was the first president elected from the Deep South since before the Civil War. The son of a prosperous peanut-farming couple, he left his Plains, Georgia, home to attend the Georgia Institute of Technology, eventually graduating from the U.S. Naval Academy. Carter served on a nuclear submarine and studied nuclear physics before returning to Georgia to run the family businesses.

He was elected to the Georgia state senate, defeated in a run for governor in 1966, then elected governor in 1970. Carter won the Democratic nomination for president in 1976, defeating incumbent Republican President Gerald Ford in November. His election as the thirty-ninth president was significant in part because he represented modern business in a region of the country that had been a backwater but was now growing at an exciting rate.

An intelligent and religious man, but without a stirring personality, Carter's integrity was never questioned but his judgment certainly was. He was blamed for weakening the country's defenses, despite the fact that his administration continued such programs as deploying the Trident submarine missile, upgrading Minuteman warheads, and developing cruise missiles. Nevertheless, among Republicans and conservative Democrats, there was a widespread belief that Carter just wasn't as frightened of the Soviet Union as he should have been. Would his Strategic Arms Limitation Talks (SALT) deal away America's strength?

At home, the economy simply refused to improve. Carter was the victim, too, of a boozing brother who became the laughingstock of the country. Inflation and the hostage crisis gave Democrats the excuse they needed to vote for a Republican, Ronald Reagan, in 1980.

Curiously enough, Carter's stature grew once out of office. There was renewed respect for one of his most popular themes, universal human rights, and he gave Habitat for Humanity, a home-building program for the poor, widespread publicity. Perhaps the man's only failing was the inability to handle or delegate the hundreds of big and little tasks expected of a chief executive.

He now heads the Carter Center at Emory University and teaches government there. He also runs Global 2000, which attacks worldwide poverty, and helps fund research for illnesses such as river blindness.

annual budget — to spend no more than it took in. Every year since 1965, those in power outspent all that was collected in taxes. To make up the difference, billions and billions of dollars were borrowed. People who wanted a balanced budget (they increased in number as the 1980s proceeded) said the government was competing with private enterprise for the money being saved by its citizens. Liberals accused conservatives of overspending on defense; conservatives believed liberals spent excessively on social programs.

What made this important? The answer was evident all across the country: Without money to invest, there were few new factories, roads, bridges, schools, technologies, or jobs. The deficit was a rutted interstate highway in Pennsylvania, an aging assembly-line in Chicago, or a leaking levee along the Mississippi River. It might also be an aircraft plant in California, with huge defense contracts but too many nonproductive employees. Money that should have gone to explore the new and repair the exist-

ing instead paid interest on funds borrowed earlier. Neither the government nor the private sector had money for investment or improvement. It went to feed the deficit.

Carter's brightest moment came in 1979 when he managed to bring the warring Middle East nations of Egypt and Israel together to sign what has come to be called the Camp David Peace Accord. Despite increasing instances of Middle Eastern terrorism, the peace treaty ended thirty years of war and mistrust in the vicinity of the Suez Canal. The accord was greeted less than enthusiastically in other parts of the region, where the United States was seen as a corrupting influence among many devout followers of Islam, the Muslims. Terrorism continued, spawned in part by extremist Muslim resentment of the U. S.

Muslims, led by conservative Islamic clergy, overthrew the shah of Iran in 1978. An ally of the United States, the shah was seen by many of his own people as one who believed Western culture and torturing enemies

The aftermath of the disastrous effort to free the American hostages in Iran in April 1980. Helicopters on a commando raid suffered technical problems due to the desert conditions. A helicopter collided with a transport plane, killing eight servicemen. Secretary of State Cyrus Vance, who had been opposed to the expedition from the start, resigned after its failure.

The unemployed stand in line in Detroit in 1980. Detroit, a center of the car manufacturing industry, was badly hit by the recession. At the beginning of the decade, Japanese cars were generally perceived as more reliable and of better quality than those produced in the U.S. In addition, most European and Japanese cars were smaller and more fuel-efficient. In response to public demand, American automakers had to rethink their policies and try to catch up with the competition.

were more important than Islam. Relations between Iran and the U.S. deteriorated to the point that militants seized the American embassy on November 4, 1979, holding its sixty-three occupants hostage. Jimmy Carter ordered a U.S. Army commando raid to free the captured Americans. The operation ended when helicopters flying toward the capital city of Tehran took in sand or otherwise malfunctioned. Eight American soldiers were killed and five wounded in the ill-fated rescue effort. Yellow ribbons sprouted on trees all across the U.S., but they were as much symbols of frustration as of hope for the safe return of the hostages.

Feelings Against Foreigners

Other things lurking below the surface of American life caused voters to be upset. Among them was the growing number of illegal immigrants in the country. A Census Bureau study released in February 1980 indicated that there might be as many as six million illegal aliens in the United States at any one time. The unemployed, and there were millions of them, resented the fact that foreigners were working, even though most foreign laborers were in unskilled, very low-paying positions no one else wanted.

Proof that immigration was out of control could be found in the report, which admitted that figures were inexact — illegal aliens could total as few as 3.5 million or as many as 12 million. Mexican-Americans read the report and called 6 million an exaggeration. They felt such studies heightened tensions over the impact of aliens, legal and otherwise, in the workforce. But there were other, uglier manifestations of the antiforeigners mood during the decade.

In Detroit, where American cars of marginal quality were coming off assembly lines, the frustration level was at an all-time high. Slow sales of U.S. cars resulted in auto industry layoffs, while sturdy, fuel efficient cars made in Japan continued to sell briskly in this country. In fact, world-wide sales of Japanese cars exceeded sales of U.S. vehicles for the first time in 1980. Japanese car sales would continue to grow throughout the decade. In Detroit in 1984, a laid-off auto worker, believing a Chinese-American to be Japanese, attacked and killed him with a baseball bat. That was the ugliest manifestation of a decade-long sentiment that included bumper stickers reading: "Unemployed? Hungry? Eat your foreign car."

Democrats Adrift

There were other frustrations among Democrats, organized labor and labor's traditional supporters. Democrats were spread all over the ideological map, from conservative blue-collar union members to antiwar activists committed to world peace. The Democratic party lacked fresh leadership and fresh ideas, and many of Lyndon Johnson's War on Poverty social plans had lost their vitality. Democrats who had worked to put their children through college were rewarded with graduates who were often Republicans. Many white Democrats weren't that excited by civil rights — an ongoing party- and labor-leadership theme. Pacifists and other left-leaning members of society were disliked by many Americans, who never forgave them for being morally right and less than patriotic over the Vietnam War.

Congressional Scandal

Liberal or conservative, several members of Congress were linked to bribery and corruption by agents from the Federal Bureau of Investigation. The story broke in February 1980 that the FBI, posing as wealthy Arab executives, had approached several members of Congress. The undercover agents offered bribes of as much as $50,000 to officials in exchange for influence of various kinds.

Eight men, seven of them Democrats, were linked to "Abscam," the FBI nickname for Arab Scam. The elected officials were recorded by hidden video cameras, happily taking the money, though one representative, Republican Richard Kelly of Florida, claimed he accepted $25,000 because he was secretly conducting an investigation of his own!

Democrat Michael Myers was the first person in over a hundred years to be expelled from Congress. The FBI offered bribes to government officials in return for influence, and eight of them were recorded on video accepting the money. The Abscam sting was bad publicity for the Democrats and harmed Arab-American relations because the FBI agents had posed as Arab businessmen.

Several of the accused had earlier troubles, leading some to wonder if the FBI was picking on the afflicted. Democratic Senator Harrison A. "Pete" Williams of New Jersey was a recovering alcoholic, while Democratic Representative John W. Jenrette of South Carolina had been implicated in a drug-smuggling ring by a friend and had a stormy personal life. Most admitted their guilt, were convicted, and left government.

One senator who had turned down the money criticized the FBI for attempting to corrupt him. But many Americans felt Congress was a big fat-cat club eagerly awaiting bribe money. Jimmy Carter was personally incorruptible, but Abscam did little to foster confidence in Democrats or in the politics of Washington. It also did little for Arab-American relations, since the FBI chose to make Arabs look like troublemakers and opportunists. The U.S. later apologized to both the Arab-American community and to its friends in the Middle East.

Economic Troubles

Jimmy Carter and the rest of America had troubles of their own. The president tried to run the country, conduct a reelection campaign, and absorb the steady stream of bad economic news. The prime rate, which is the rate of interest banks charge their biggest and best customers, spiraled upward in the late winter of 1980. Like a wound that kept growing larger, interest on loans climbed from 15.25 percent at the start of 1980 to 17.25 percent two months later. Sales of homes and cars were flat. The average American knew that if manufacturers and businesses were being charged high rates, those high rates would be passed along. He or she realized that high rates meant no economic expansion or job creation.

Similarly, the U.S. balance of trade continued to climb in favor of foreign trading partners. Japan, Europe, and the rest of the world were selling the U.S. much more than they were buying from America. Money was leaving the country at the rate of about $4 billion a month. Several products invented in the United States, such as television sets and typewriters, were made so inexpensively overseas that plants producing them here ceased to exist. All this and more played on the minds of voters, though Carter did well enough in Democratic primaries to be renominated by his party.

Reagan to the Rescue

To the rescue came actor-turned-politician Ronald Reagan. Following a career in the movies and as host of two long-running television series, Reagan was elected governor of California in 1966. He remained active in conservative Republican politics afterward, biding his time until the country swung around to his point of view. Swing it finally did, willing to try something different in the wake of the mediocrity it had witnessed in the 1970s. On November 4, 1980, Ronald Reagan and his running mate George Bush beat the incumbents Jimmy Carter and Walter Mondale in a landslide.

Texas oil men celebrated with a cake baked in the shape of Capitol Hill and labeled "Ours." The inauguration ceremonies were lavish in the

"A very conservative Republican can't win in a national election."

Gerald Ford, 1980

extreme, as well-dressed people ate shrimp at huge Union Station tables while homeless residents of Washington crashed the party to gnaw on catered food alongside the VIPs. Furs, private planes, and costly jewelry were in evidence everywhere. So

The Nation's Worries

It would be wrong, however, to view such events as pure party politics. Proof that politics didn't matter much to Americans could be found in

many expensive limousines were rented that there was a shortage, not only in the District of Columbia itself, but along a large section of the Eastern Seaboard as well. The 1981 Reagan presidential inaugural turned out to be easily the most expensive ever, "a celebration of the 'haves,'" according to one critic.

their dismal voting records in local, state, and national elections. What, then, was important as the country began a new decade? Carter was right: There *was* a crisis of confidence. Confidence wavered over more than finances and interest rates.

A major concern was Social Security and whether it would continue to

Ronald Reagan is sworn in as president of the United States of America on January 20, 1981. His wife and Jimmy Carter look on.

A homeless man lies on a bench in the snow outside the White House in November 1987. The problem of homelessness in major cities increased alarmingly during the decade.

be a reliable method of caring for aging, retired workers. The program had been put in place in the 1930s and, since then, had given back money to most elderly and retired citizens to help care for them in their old age. But people were living longer, Social Security was showing signs of strain, and no one wanted to be in the enforced savings program if those savings were all used up by the time they retired. A vocal minority believed it was time to end the program, though this was not taken seriously. Older people, led by Senator Claude Pepper and represented by the American Association of Retired Persons (AARP) and other groups, threatened to vote out of office anyone who tampered with Social Security.

There was the sneaking suspicion that citizens at several levels, from welfare mothers to fat cats, were getting free rides at the expense of the middle class. Literal proof of such activity turned up in newspapers, where there were reports of welfare clients taking cabs to and from meetings with their social workers. Salaries for people in charge of major corporations were dozens of times the salaries of the average worker for such corporations — even though these businesses might be losing money. As stories of inflated contracts for professional athletes and others were read or seen by the public, resentment grew.

The nation's major cities were in decline. Troubles seemed to intensify with population growth, as immigrants took jobs at the bottom of the economic ladder and began their fight up each rung. Ethnic groups were tossed together in a bewildering stew that fed the crime rate. Crowded conditions, particularly in public housing, indicated that a free place to live might cause as many woes as it solved. The number of people without any home at all continued to grow. For middle-class whites who continued to flee to the suburbs, today's big-city crisis threatened to become tomorrow's new suburban problem.

Guns, drugs, and crime spread and caused alarm. Crime had been a problem for years and was not about to go away. More and more citizens backed maximum sentences and no parole for offenders, but the cost of imprisonment was high and climbing. During the decade, the United States had a higher percentage of its people locked up than did such controversial places as China or South Africa. Ironically, many of the same people who cried the loudest for crime control did not want to give up their guns. Though repeated surveys showed most Americans wanted gun control, it did not happen.

The decline of quality and inventiveness in American products bothered consumers and manufacturers alike. Productivity — the rate at which a company makes a product — was stagnant. In contrast, Japanese manufacturers were creating products in a fraction of the time it took Americans. Worse, the time between when a product was conceived and when it came off the assembly-line was much shorter in Japan than in the United States. Some Americans argued that their country should not have rebuilt Japan so effectively following World War II. But that did not address shoddy workmanship, inefficient, outdated designs, and other problems in American plants and factories.

A drop in student test scores and, logically, a decline in American education in general, was equally disturbing. Too many high school graduates could barely find their own country on a map, were unaware that New Mexico was part of the United States, and could not balance a checkbook. More than 10 percent were functionally illiterate. Teachers were blamed, and they, in turn, blamed families in homes where education was not valued.

Almost everyone was critical of television, often linking it to some of these troubles. One newspaper headline, citing a scientific study, used very unscientific terms to assess the situation: "TV makes kids fat and mean," it said. Yet because people had less leisure time, they also had less energy. Turning on the television was often a convenient means of escape.

> "The idea has been established over the past ten years that almost every service that someone might need in life ought to be provided by the government .... We reject that notion."
>
> Ronald Reagan

Intuitively, many perceived a lack of pride in the country. There were other matters that defied simple solutions as well, from abortion to the environment. Discussing them only seemed to further alienate one citizen from another. Something had to be done but was Reagan the man to do it?

Republican politicians symbolically smash a Toshiba radio with sledgehammers in July 1987 to protest the sale of strategic submarine technology by a Toshiba subsidiary to the Soviet Union. Many Americans were outraged that Japan would sell defense-related technology to a nation still considered America's enemy.

the Democratic president had done little to improve the average American's economic lot. Big business lined up behind the Republican candidate and voters endorsed his ideas.

Minutes after Reagan's inauguration on January 20, 1981, the fifty-two Americans still held hostage in Iran were released, following a compromise in which the U.S. agreed to return $8 billion of Iran's frozen assets. It was later shown that Reagan advisors pledged to send arms to Iran in exchange for the release of the prisoners, but only after the inauguration.

Surviving a Bullet

Clearly, many in the country were pleased that Ronald Reagan had taken the helm. And, an incident just weeks after the inauguration solidified the image of the new president in the hearts of his people. Stepping toward his limousine in Washington on the soggy afternoon of March 30, 1981, Reagan was shot by a deranged young man named John Hinckley. No one died in the half a dozen shots that were fired, but Reagan was

In the assassination attempt on President Reagan in March 1981, the president's press secretary, James Brady (on the ground at right), and a policeman lie wounded. In the background on the right, the would-be assassin, John Hinckley, is held by police and security agents.

Alexander M. Haig.

Alexander M. Haig served Ronald Reagan as secretary of state, but not for long. The man who had helped hold the White House together during the demise of President Richard M. Nixon quickly became an outcast among the high rollers and opportunists who blew into Washington in 1981.

Haig shared the new president's distrust of communism, but he was not a fanatic. A graduate of West Point, he had served capably in Vietnam, and, as a general, had been  supreme commander of America's forces based in Europe. Reagan named him secretary of state without the two knowing each other well. Haig lasted until July 1982.

Reagan insiders who grew to dislike Haig included Caspar Weinberger, secretary of defense, and William P. Clark, national security advisor. Haig favored a soft line toward Israel, while they criticized the Israelis for their invasion of Lebanon. There were other points of contention, such as the U.S. decision to ban pipeline equipment sales to the Soviet Union. While he viewed troubles in Central America with the same alarm as other White House officials, he gradually lost favor.

Unfortunately for the general, his forty years of service to his country are overshadowed by a couple of low moments. Minutes after the president was shot in 1981, Haig told the media, "I'm in charge" when he wasn't. He ran unsuccessfully for president in 1988, his campaign probably colored by the public's fuzzy notion that he had been a part of either the Watergate or Iran-contra affairs, although neither was the case.

struck in the chest, and James Brady, his press secretary, sustained a serious head wound.

Advisors quickly reported that the president was in no danger, which was a lie. The bullet had punctured a lung and lodged near his heart. But Reagan got out of bed and waved and smiled from his hospital window to anxiously waiting fans. The assassination attempt made him even more popular, fixing the president in the public mind as a man who could not be stopped by mere bullets. Able to return to work several weeks later, he was even cordially received by opposition Democrats.

Controlling the Skies

The first group to defy the president was PATCO, the air-traffic controllers' union, which planned to strike for better hours and wages. Though they had been warned not to do so by the administration, most of the thirteen thousand union members staged a strike, defying Reagan. The president fired them all on August 5, 1981, and, despite fears for the safety of air passengers, replacements were quickly called in. Support for the president's decisive action was overwhelming in the business community, but public employees and labor unions opposed it, as did many private citizens.

But facts and figures also weighed against Reagan during his first term. In 1982, for example, the U.S. automotive industry reported its lowest sales in twenty years. Analysts attributed the dismal figures to high interest rates, high unemployment, and the fear of unemployment for those with jobs. The latter was no idle worry: In 1982 unemployment averaged 9.7 percent and approached 11 percent as that year drew to a close. Figures failed to tell the whole story, as numerous unemployed adults eventually became discouraged and simply quit looking for work, thereby ceasing to register as even a statistic.

The prime interest rate finally began to decline early in 1983, dropping below 11 percent for the first time in months. Unemployment also peaked as a bipartisan jobs bill finally was passed, despite little help from Reagan. Also passed over Ronald Reagan's veto was the decision to punish South Africa with economic sanctions for its policy of racial segregation. Reagan never found favor with African-Americans, no doubt because of his hands-off attitude toward both the weak economy and South Africa. In contrast, the president's leadership gained the support of many former Democrats, among them a young economics advisor named David Stockman.

Supply-Side Economics, Politics, and Reelection

David Stockman had grown up on a farm in Michigan. Originally a Democrat, he had studied economics and decided that supply-side theory was what America needed. The theory involved decreasing taxes so that the well-to-do could invest; the results would "trickle down" the economic ladder to the average American. Stockman and others put together numbers to "prove" the advantages of supply-siding, but the young advisor later admitted to *Atlantic Monthly* magazine that the theory did not work! Stockman, whose star quickly fell, was correct: Inflation eased, but there was a deep recession during the 1981-83 period, and much of the good news Republicans found was merely the result of a change in the way the numbers were presented.

Democratic votes certainly reflected their acceptance of supply-side economics. Not much opposition was voiced to Reagan's economic program, which included the largest budget and tax cuts in U.S. history, as well as a Social Security reform bill designed to keep that program healthy. Despite backing from members of both parties, there was concern that the country would be hurt by cutting taxes as it dramatically jacked up the defense budget. Reagan promised "safety nets" under social programs for the poorest and least capable members of society, particularly children. But as he was making such pledges, his people were trying to get catsup listed as a vegetable so that they would have to give less free food to the hungry!

Who was hurt by the hard line on welfare and related social programs? Among its most evident victims were single mothers whose lack of support in the decade made poverty a certainty for them. Thomas "Tip" O'Neill, a Democrat and the Speaker of the House in the early

> *"None of us really knows what's going on with all these numbers."*
>
> David Stockman, Federal Budget Director, 1981

> *"When it comes to giving tax breaks to the wealthy of this country, the president has a heart of gold."*
>
> Thomas ("Tip") O'Neill, Speaker of the U.S. House of Representatives

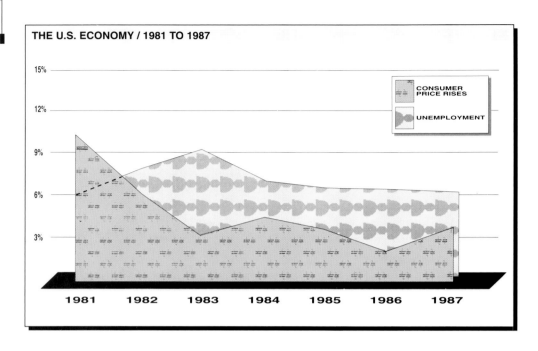

THE U.S. ECONOMY / 1981 TO 1987

After two years of rising unemployment, President Reagan's policies began to turn the tide by 1983. Increased business created more jobs while inflation fell between 1984 and 1986.

"Waiting for supply-side economics to work is like leaving landing lights on for Amelia Earhart."

Walter Heller, economist

1980s, tells of meeting with Reagan and reporting on a single mother from his Massachusetts district who was working and trying to get an education at the same time. The federal program that kept her afloat was being cut, and she would have to quit school. Reagan told O'Neill he would find a way to get the woman money, oblivious to the fact that O'Neill was informing the president of an entire class of people being cut off at the knees.

Meanwhile, the president came up for reelection with the economy gaining strength and inflation subsiding. Democrats nominated former Vice President Walter Mondale of Minnesota, who named U.S. House of Representatives member Geraldine Ferraro of New York as his running mate. Ferraro was the first woman ever picked to run for high office by a major party. While both Democrats were seen as acceptable, Mondale appeared weak and there were allegations about Ferraro's friends, relatives,

and ethics. The Mondale-Ferraro ticket won only in Minnesota and the District of Columbia. Ronald Reagan became, at seventy-three, the oldest person ever elected to the nation's highest post.

Foreign Policy

Like his domestic economic policy, Reagan's foreign policy was remarkably simple — the United States would uphold freedom and protect its allies everywhere. The president saw the Soviet Union as "an evil empire," yet he was easier on it than his predecessor, Jimmy Carter. During Ronald Reagan's watch, the Soviets imposed martial law in Poland, shot down a Korean airliner that had strayed over Soviet airspace, and funneled arms to Syria in the Lebanese war with Israel. Anti-Soviet hard-liners, often Republicans, seethed with indignation but kept quiet.

Walter Mondale.

Early in his career, someone asked Walter Frederick ("Fritz") Mondale if he ever wanted to run for president. "Naw," Mondale is quoted as saying, "I don't want to spend two years of my life in motels."

Mondale was born in Ceylon, Minnesota, in 1928. He graduated with honors from the University of Minnesota, then successfully attended its law school. After serving in the U.S. Army, law clerking, and working in private practice, Mondale won the race for state attorney general and served four years before running for the U.S. Senate. A Democrat, he served in the Senate from 1964 to 1977.

Jimmy Carter persuaded Mondale to be his running mate for the 1976 presidential race. The two were just different enough to succeed: Carter was an engineer and a farmer, Mondale an attorney. Only Mondale had Washington experience, where his voting record proved him to be a consistent liberal. He served President Carter well for four years in what has been called the world's worst job. He and the president were beaten in a landslide by Ronald Reagan and George Bush in the 1980 election.

Mondale was persuaded to run for president in 1984. Certainly, there have been more enthusiastic candidates. But he did point out the chinks in Ronald Reagan's armor while sounding the traditional Democratic call for jobs — to be supplied by the federal government as a last resort. Perhaps the most noteworthy event of Mondale's campaign was his choice of running mate. He picked Geraldine Ferraro, a New Yorker who had earned the respect of many feminists.

It wasn't enough. Ronald Reagan didn't blow Mondale away in debates as had been expected, but the Republicans harped on a few key themes: To stay with the Reagan economic plan, to steer clear of liberals such as Mondale, and to maintain a strong defense by voting for the GOP. After the race, Mondale returned to Minnesota to work. He would be named ambassador to Japan, America's largest trading partner, in 1993.

Walter Mondale with his 1984 presidential campaign running mate, Geraldine Ferraro.

Perhaps Reagan's biggest brush with disaster took place in Lebanon in 1983. A total of 241 U.S. Marines, sent to keep peace in war-torn Beirut, were killed when a terrorist drove an explosives-laden truck into their barracks. The remaining marines were withdrawn offshore, but there was no mention of punishing whoever was responsible for the deaths of American soldiers. Reagan was equally meek in dealing with Libyan terrorist attacks, though there was an American air raid on Libya, and also with the Soviets, who were still fighting in Afghanistan. Unlike

Teddy Roosevelt, the president who spoke softly and carried a big stick, Reagan spoke loudly while holding a small twig.

Nevertheless, he held summit meetings with Soviet leader Mikhail Gorbachev in 1985 in Geneva, in 1986 in Iceland, and in 1987 in Washington. The final meeting resulted in an historic treaty eliminating short- and medium-range missiles from Europe. In May 1988, President Reagan visited Moscow. He chided the Soviets over their dismal human rights record and met with dissidents. The president's admirers would claim that his tough stand on weaponry and his relentless defense buildup forced the Soviet Union to the treaty table, while detractors would give Mikhail Gorbachev most of the credit.

Following revelations that the president had been willing to subvert the Constitution in the 1986 Iran-contra scandal (see Chapter 7), his popularity declined. The 1986 congressional elections saw Democrats make gains in both houses. No one was in the mood to impeach a dodderingly old president, so Reagan maintained his "watch" over the country for the last two years in relative isolation. He continued to perform at public functions, from the memorial service for the *Challenger* astronauts to numerous photo opportunities for the media.

Overpowering the Media

Reagan and his people took an uncompromising line toward the news media, and the news media fell

The French Embassy was one of the buildings hit in the U.S. air raid on Tripoli, Libya, on April 15, 1986. The attack was a retaliation against the bombing of a West Berlin discotheque that was frequented by American service personnel. That outrage was believed to have been perpetrated by Libya.

all over itself trying to please the chief executive. Called the "Teflon president" because problems slid off him, Reagan was able to control what was said about him using a combination of his own likeability and the careful orchestration of events by his handlers. In contrast to the tough stance taken against presidents such as Lyndon Johnson and Richard Nixon, the news media played dead around Ronald Reagan. The fact that many of his appointees resigned because they were criminals says more about their own ineptness than about investigative journalism, which had virtually ceased to exist.

Most news, such as the behavior of First Lady Nancy Reagan, came from within. Warned that putting pressure on clothing designers to furnish her with free apparel was illegal, Nancy admitted in her husband's second term that she had "broken the little promise I made to myself" about the practice. In fact, she had broken the law. More controversial was her dependence on astrologers. Secretary of the Treasury and White House Chief of Staff, Donald Regan, who fell out of favor with the first lady and left the administration, revealed that Nancy set appointments for herself and the president based on her horoscope! Fundamentalist Christians, who had supported the Reagans all along, were shocked.

A Distinct President

But what made Ronald Reagan different to Richard M. Nixon was his ability to disregard anything that collided with his views. During both his terms, for example, there was an active and growing antinuclear movement.

Huge rallies in New York City, in Britain, and elsewhere in Europe were complemented by two thousand women setting up camp near the Seneca Army Depot in upstate New York to protest the arms race. The Seabrook, New Hampshire, nuclear power-generating plant was the target of outrage of people from all over New England — yet the president simply paid the entire movement no heed. Perhaps future presidents will be able to learn from Ronald Reagan's incredible ability to pay selective attention to issues.

President Reagan, on his visit to Moscow in May 1988, stands under a bust of Lenin at Moscow University as he addresses students. He was welcomed by the Soviet people, met several dissidents, and criticized the Soviet Union's human rights record. However, he had moved a long way from his description, earlier in the decade, of the Soviet Union as "the focus of evil in the modern world."

Was Ronald Reagan's presidency good for the country? Experts disagree. His biggest contribution was that he made it acceptable to be proud to be American, and after the embarrassment of Watergate and the failed hostage rescue, this was very important for U.S. morale. His lack of interest in the environment, the growing homeless population, and the exploding drug problem made virtually everyone skeptical of his economic and social policies. But there is little doubt that he was something new and different, and that America in the 1980s hung its hopes on his shoulders.

The Great Peace March for Global Nuclear Disarmament reaches the White House on November 15, 1986, after a thirty-five-hundred-mile journey from Los Angeles that had taken eight months. Here, a poster protests the Strategic Defense Initiative, or "Star Wars" program, an attempt to construct a shield that would be placed in space in order to destroy Soviet missiles before they struck American targets. Most people outside the Reagan administration considered it technologically impossible and outrageously expensive.

CHAPTER 3
Concerns Old and New

Even at the age of fifty-eight, Rock Hudson was a handsome man. The film star had played all-American heroes for years, wooing and winning Hollywood's top actresses. He had starred in adventures and romantic comedies throughout the 1960s and 1970s. Lately, he had enjoyed success on television in a detective series and in a prime-time soap opera. But now in the spring of 1984, he was worried. A purple spot on his neck seemed to be spreading. A piece of tissue was nicked from the spot by Hudson's doctor, and test results on it were grim — the actor had skin cancer. Worse, the type of cancer indicated that Rock Hudson was suffering from AIDS.

AIDS, Acquired Immune Deficiency Syndrome, a hideous disease, first became widely known in the 1980s. It continues to stalk the world today. Had government action been taken more quickly, the epidemic might have killed far fewer here and abroad. Figures from 1990 show that AIDS has caused the deaths of more than 150,000 U.S. residents. Even more carry the deadly HIV virus that causes the disease. No cure has yet been found.

The disease, which is always fatal, surfaced in Central Africa in the mid-1970s. People there were coming down with rare forms of pneumonia, cancer, allergies, rashes, blindness, running sores, and growths, accompanied by high fever, night sweats, brain damage, and a slow, agonizing end. Europeans working in Africa, often as doctors and nurses, contracted the HIV virus and returned home as carriers. AIDS spread to the United States as well. New York and San Francisco quickly had dozens of AIDS patients who were primarily gay, sexually active men. Soon, they were joined by others.

Numerous Haitians living in Haiti and in America showed symptoms. Doctors gradually learned that the Haitians had been infected by residents of their island who had worked in Africa. Others caught AIDS after

Actor Robert Blake standing in front of the AIDS quilt at a press conference. This quilt, begun in 1986, commemorates in personalized quilted squares the many thousands who have died from AIDS. Each panel is made by friends or relatives in remembrance of those individuals. This memorial has been displayed in whole or in part (because of its huge size) in the U.S. and all over the world. Sadly, the quilt grows daily with new panels.

sharing hypodermic needles contaminated by HIV-positive drug addicts, by being born to a drug user, or by receiving a tainted blood transfusion as a result of an illness. Exchanging bodily fluids through sex could also pass the disease to its next victim.

AIDS is as deadly a disease as anything ever inflicted upon humanity. It destroys the body's ability to fight off afflictions seldom seen in human beings. Consequently, people with AIDS suffer from cancers previously known only in isolated ethnic groups or in birds or animals, or from strange diseases that fill the lungs with millions of churning organisms. By the time French researchers isolated the HIV virus that causes the disease in 1984, almost two thousand Americans were dead and more than twenty-five hundred were infected.

The Politics of AIDS

Like many things in the 1980s, AIDS took on a political spin. Gay activists blamed the conservative Reagan administration for not immediately pouring millions of research dollars into a fund to combat the disease. Administration officials, some of whom agreed that AIDS was a desperate emergency, were forced to remain silent because religious conservatives (who were Reagan supporters) saw the disease as a punishment from God for homosexuality. Conservative Christian influence forced the Department of Health and Human Services to drag its feet for several years as the disease spread, despite the efforts of Dr. C. Everett Koop, the surgeon general.

And spread it did. Since blood banks could not screen out all of their products for the virus, because the tests weren't definitive, people entering hospitals for unrelated problems could leave with transfusions of AIDS-tainted blood. Plus, AIDS could be carried by an infected person for years before a symptom appeared. Eventually, gay bathhouses were closed, better blood tests were designed, used needles were disposed of, and a cure was aggressively sought.

The influence of AIDS has been immense. Cautious adults no longer participate in casual sex without using

Rock Hudson, with his one-time co-star Doris Day, in July 1985 in Paris, where he was being treated for AIDS. He died that year, the first famous person to die of the disease since it was discovered in 1982.

condoms. Condoms, by the late 1980s, were sold more openly in most supermarkets. Students were warned in school about AIDS, even though few adults were eager to explain how the disease was passed along sexually.

Rock Hudson's death is important because it signaled to the country that AIDS wasn't just a disease that killed faceless strangers. President Ronald Reagan did not publicly mention the AIDS epidemic until 1987 — long after activists such as actress Elizabeth Taylor began a crusade for more government attention. This reluctance to talk about AIDS as a problem was ironic in view of the fact that Reagan and the first lady were personal friends of Hudson. Hudson, pianist Liberace, tennis star Arthur Ashe, and many other celebrities and ordinary people became the plague's victims.

Many became unwilling centers of attention. In Tampa, Florida, in 1987, three young hemophiliac brothers infected with the HIV virus were ordered admittance to the local public school by a judge. Despite assurances that the disease could not be passed on by casual contact, parents boycotted the school. After the hemophiliac family received death threats and their home was damaged by a suspicious fire, they left town.

Few Americans became hysterical over the disease, though events would try their patience. Hypodermic needles, the small instruments used to inject drugs and other substances, washed up on beaches all over the country's coasts. At a time when everyone, from surgical nurses to dental hygienists, was pulling on masks and gloves, these potentially deadly syringes apparently were being dumped almost anywhere by private

haulers collecting hospital and clinic waste. Several East Coast beaches had to be temporarily closed and the refuse removed.

The syringes and other scary debris also may have washed ashore from the increasing numbers of garbage-laden barges that were shipped out of the crowded New York City area. One such vessel, a thirty-one hundred-ton barge, left Long Island, New York, on March 3, 1987, headed for a landfill in North Carolina. Carolinians refused the cargo, as did four other states, plus Mexico, Belize, and the Bahamas. After a four-month, six thousand-mile round trip, the garbage was burned in Brooklyn. Waste from the East Coast was hauled to landfills as far away as the Midwest.

Alzheimer's Disease

If AIDS panicked the sexually active, Alzheimer's disease haunted older Americans. With age, everyone loses some of their memory. But this brain killer of unknown origin and without cure wiped out recall and made the elderly irritable, disoriented, incapable of following directions, or even eating, dressing, or using the toilet. Like AIDS, Alzheimer's disease resulted in gradual and premature death. By the decade's end, four million Americans suffered from the disease, and thousands were dead.

What caused the affliction? Was this a disease that had always been around but now was noticed because so many people lived to such old age? Causes were checked and discarded — everything from aluminum cookware to underarm deodorant was blamed for the terrible failing of aging

CULTURE AND SOCIETY

For further information see primary source entries on pages

11: 1469-70, 1509-10, 1516-18, 1520;
12: 1613-17, 1671-73, 1719-21

A garbage-laden barge from New York City is inspected in Key West, Florida, in May 1987, by federal environmental officials wearing protective clothing. They are using monitoring equipment to see if it is hazardous. Eventually, after many states and some other countries refused to take the cargo, it was returned to Brooklyn to be burnt. The carrying of garbage in barges like this is believed to have contributed to the pollution, including deadly syringes, washing ashore on America's eastern coastline.

brains. Autopsies revealed that the disease, named after a scientist who discovered it in 1907, left plaque deposits and tangles in the brains of its victims. By 1989, researchers suspected that Alzheimer's disease could be inherited through human genes but no cure was in sight.

Both AIDS and Alzheimer's brought up troubling questions. What would all of this additional health care and supervision do to already stretched governmental budgets? What was to be done with an AIDS or an Alzheimer's patient dumped at a hospital without insurance, relatives, or money? How much care should be given a baby born with AIDS? Did the addicted deserve attention? If so, how much? With

modern medicine able to keep the dying alive and suffering for long periods of time, more and more Americans quietly signed legal forms stating that no extraordinary life-support measures were to be taken if and when they became fatally ill.

A related issue caused a different kind of concern: Should researchers inform people born with genes known to carry or make more likely the onset of a specific disease? Millions of people might possess a gene that thickened arteries with cholesterol and caused premature heart attacks, for example. What was the role of the researcher and the physician in this potential, but not always deadly, problem? Did or did not the

Dr. C. Everett Koop.

Nothing could have pleased conservative Republicans more than to have Dr. C. Everett Koop serve as the U.S. Surgeon General. A widely read surgeon of impeccable medical skills, he despised abortion and was a deeply religious Christian. Several liberal organizations threw tantrums when he was nominated in 1982.

Koop turned out to be a disappointment to some conservatives, some liberals, and everyone else who wanted him to put his ideology above his integrity and his professionalism. For example, he sent President Reagan a report on the psychological effects on women who have had an abortion. Conceived inside the White House, the report was supposed to "prove" how damaging an abortion could be on the mother. Instead, many women said their abortion was the best thing they ever did, and Koop reported the findings with 100 percent accuracy.

The Brooklyn native was savaged by U.S. Senator Jesse Helms for his uncompromising attack on the evils of tobacco. Koop condemned the U.S. for exporting tobacco products while he damned the use of tobacco in any kind of public or government building. The Reagan Administration sabotaged Koop's attempts to make the government's anti-tobacco campaign even stronger than it already was.

Koop also spoke out on AIDS, turning once again to his professional rather than his personal opinion. Once an opponent of legalized homosexuality, the large man with the Amish-style beard came to view gays as the unlucky victims of the disease. His advocacy of the use of condoms was due to the fact that 70 percent of teens are sexually active and, when you tell them to abstain, "they laugh at you."

Koop was big hearted enough to want to save even those who laughed. He also was a doctor and a man of science above all else, as his many books, papers, articles, and speeches proved. Unlike other cabinet-level posts, the surgeon general is nominated every four years. In 1990, President George Bush chose not to renominate the controversial physician.

---

sons and daughters of persons suffering from apparently inherited illnesses have a right to know about their own bodies? There were no easy answers to these ethical questions.

Guns, Kids, Drugs, and Crime

Neither AIDS nor Alzheimer's disease, nor even a hit-and-run vehicle, struck as quickly and as senselessly as the bullets that flew more and more, not only in America's inner cities but in suburbs and smaller towns, too. The connection between guns and drugs was a strong one, with six million Americans using cocaine in 1985 — just before smokeable crack cocaine was introduced.

Cocaine laid low the meek and the mighty. Len Bias, a University of Maryland basketball star, celebrated being drafted by the Boston Celtics on June 19, 1986, by getting high. He died of a heart attack caused by cocaine. Eight days later, Don Rogers, a professional football player with the Cleveland Browns, took cocaine shortly before his wedding and died almost immediately. The two athletes became symbols, and important ones: If cocaine could kill even the most fit, who was safe from its effects?

Crack cocaine changed the nature of inner-city neighborhoods. Kids had always been warned to stay away from boarded-up, condemned houses because desperate people might lurk inside. But those inside crack houses became more desperate, larger in number, and willing to commit crime to feed the crack habit. Crack was a rocklike piece of cocaine, formerly available only as powder that was snorted up the nose. But the rocks could be lighted and smoked in a dope pipe, creating an instant high. Cocaine taken in either form was

Edna Buchanan.

No American city better represented the violent side of the decade than Miami, Florida. And no one conveyed the sense of hot, steamy danger and death better than Edna Buchanan, police reporter for the *Miami Herald*.

Born in New Jersey in 1939, Buchanan, unlike most rookie reporters, applied for her first newspaper job without having studied journalism. For five years, she learned on the job, doing anything asked of her at a small Florida daily newspaper. The *Herald* hired her in 1970, and by 1973, she began to cover crime.

Buchanan has become so famous for her reporting that she is known by her first name in southern Florida. "Did you see what Edna wrote this morning?" is heard on the job, over dinner, and wherever her paper is delivered. And no wonder — her sentences are punchy, riveting, darkly funny, or all those things and more.

One example is the story of a man who was killed after walking into a fast-food chicken restaurant one evening. Buchanan's story begins this way: "Gary Robinson died hungry."

The reporter, who won a Pulitzer Prize in 1986, was not taken seriously by some police officers at first. Tall and blonde, she was shown the most grisly photos and told the most lurid tales by police. Buchanan listened and learned, turning terrible events into stories that held the attention of the state and, quite often, the nation. She claims to be lucky, but she earned the respect of cops and readers alike with her writing and reporting skills.

Miami's stories test the imagination. Buchanan has told of a naked man who threw a severed head at police, of a man who killed eight persons because he felt that a welding shop had not properly fixed his bicycle, of drug peddlers, repeat rapists, and serial killers.

She has written four books, three of them nonfiction. Her first book, *Carr: Five Years of Rape and Murder,* was widely praised because Buchanan was able to get inside the head of serial rapist Robert F. Carr III and convey how the criminal mind works. Her nonfiction articles have appeared in magazines such as *Cosmopolitan, Family Circle,* and *Rolling Stone.* Walt Disney Productions purchased film rights for her second nonfiction book, *The Corpse Had a Familiar Face.*

Buchanan is best known for being tough but sympathetic. She frequently gains the confidence of a victim's next of kin, who knows that Edna will tell the story exactly as it happened, in a way no one else can.

equally lethal, but crack, with its more dangerous but intense high, held a special attraction in the inner city where people felt they had less to lose.

Inner-city blacks tended to use crack and suburban whites tended to use cocaine in its powdered form. But because of racism, blacks found themselves facing years and years in prison, whereas whites and others who were

There were strong links among gangs, guns, and drugs. Gangs had been a nationwide problem in the 1950s but had declined in the 1960s, except in places such as New York, Los Angeles, and Chicago. There, they convinced the authorities they were socially conscious, opening up storefront operations, supposedly to help their neighbors. But the gangs

caught with the powder were handed comparatively light sentences — shorter jail terms and lesser fines. Arrests were staggering in number. Los Angeles police alone in 1988 arrested fifty-five thousand people for possession and eight thousand for dealing, much of it crack cocaine. A single courageous undercover cop in New York City was responsible for the arrest of fifteen hundred accused crack users or sellers that same year.

continued to threaten small businesses with violence if they weren't paid off. When gangs reemerged in Los Angeles in the early 1980s, experts were not surprised.

Authorities were shocked at the level of indiscriminate violence practiced by the new gangs. Drive-by shootings wiped out innocent bystanders almost as often as the hail of bullets felled someone the gang intended to hit. Gang members (there

Officers of the Los Angeles police department arrest suspected gang members as part of a massive antigang operation in 1988. Since starting up early in the decade, Los Angeles gangs had established branches in other cities, and drugs flowed freely across the country.

The shooting of an African-American youth by police officers in Miami in 1982 led to riots. Here, looters drove a stolen car through steel doors into a meat market and removed meat and food-processing machines.

could be hundreds in a single gang) identified themselves by flashing signs: They held their fingers and fists in secret, symbolic ways. Those who failed to flash the right sign or gave the wrong sign sometimes paid for their ignorance or defiance with their lives. The gangs, which could be black, brown, yellow, or white, male or female, financed the purchase of guns and cars by selling drugs. At times, they were better armed than the law officers who tried to monitor their terrifying behavior.

Once a gang established a foothold, drugs flowed into the new territory. Kids of all races, fascinated with the "gangsta rap" of sinister black entertainers dressed in sports clothing, took on the look of gang members. Schools moved to banish hats, bandanas, or other paraphernalia that hinted at gang membership. The record industry wasn't much help — a flash of emotion on an inner-city street one month could be blaring out of cassette recorders across the country the next.

The violence continued. Statistics

Gangs Branch Out

Even more worrisome, Los Angeles gangs established branches. Cities such as Phoenix, San Francisco, Portland, Denver, and Kansas City became sites for gang organizing.

showed that African-American young men were particularly victimized by gang activity. But because bullets flew everywhere, there were plenty of dead African-American women and children, too. Though whites outnumber blacks in this country by a ratio of more than six to one, the number of deaths by homicide or fatal intervention of law enforcement were equal. In other equally frightening statistics, males of all races were four times as likely as females to be killed with a gun or by the police. While cars became safer and automobile deaths declined by one-third in the 1980s, gun deaths soared. The most common cause of death among American males ages twenty-five through thirty-four was gunfire.

Public reaction to the increased use of firearms by children and young adults was strange. Some armed themselves, despite the fact that the gun they legally purchased over the counter probably had less firepower than the automatic and semiautomatic weapons carried by young hoodlums.

Others campaigned for the registration of handguns. San Francisco and Morton Grove, a Chicago suburb, banned handguns entirely. But Kennesaw, Georgia, required the head of every household to own a firearm! With each drive-by shooting, more Americans wanted handguns eliminated. Had it not been for a continuous campaign by the National Rifle Association, handgun possession might have been outlawed in the 1980s.

Yet legislation would have come too late to save the hundreds of people mowed down by well-armed, deranged individuals in post offices, office buildings, and restaurants. One who survived a senseless shooting to work for gun control was James Brady. Shot in the head and perma-

James Brady was permanently disabled in an assassination attempt on Ronald Reagan's life in 1981 while serving as press secretary. Brady and his wife, Sarah, led the campaign for gun control. Here Brady, with Sarah and two Democratic senators, is about to testify before a Senate Judiciary subcommittee on handgun legislation. Brady called Congress "gutless" about regulating the sale of handguns.

nently disabled in 1981 with Ronald Reagan while serving as the president's press secretary, Brady and his wife, Sarah, began a nationwide drive to eliminate easy access to guns. Politicians opposing gun control probably had a tough time looking Brady in the eye as he worked from his wheelchair on Capitol Hill in the 1980s.

the majority favored a woman's right to choose whether to have an abortion, a very large, vocal minority was against the practice.

Actually, the Supreme Court had ruled as far back as 1973 that a state could not prevent a woman from having an abortion in the first six months of her pregnancy. While it tightened

Members of the National Organization for Women (NOW) link hands to prevent antiabortion protesters (in the background) from disrupting their rally in Denver in June 1986. Although President Reagan was against a woman's right to have an abortion, and there were many religious groups active in opposing it, abortion continued to be legal throughout the decade.

The Abortion Issue

Foes of abortion, who thought Ronald Reagan would outlaw the procedure, turned out to be too optimistic. Reagan consistently campaigned to stop abortion, but he took little direct action. In fact, in nominating Sandra Day O'Connor as the country's first female U.S. Supreme Court justice in 1981, he placed on the court a person who believed women should have control over their own bodies. Though surveys showed throughout the eighties that

requirements in 1989, it did not overturn the 1973 *Roe v. Wade* decision, which legalized abortion across the country. Instead, it gave states the right to regulate abortion, which Pennsylvania did three months later by ordering counseling prior to an abortion. Resentment over abortion grew among some Roman Catholics and Fundamentalist Christians. Antiabortion groups such as Operation Rescue were determined to shut down Planned Parenthood, which discussed abortion as an option, and to close clinics offering the procedure. Picketing and passive resistance were used with varying degrees of success in the late 1980s, though hundreds of abortions continued to be performed daily.

Radon and Other Woes

There were additional worries. The fear of radon, an odorless, colorless gas, swept the country during the decade. Homeowners in a broad swath from North Dakota to the Atlantic Ocean were told that many of their homes contained excessive amounts of the gas, which was known to cause cancer. Numerous Americans called in experts to ventilate their basements. Some municipalities enforced a radon check whenever a house was sold. The federal Environmental Protection Agency (EPA) set the safe level of radon in a residence at four picocuries — which told the average homeowner nothing at all.

Another carcinogen, tobacco, declined in importance as a crop during the decade. Strong warnings stated that

Supporters of the proposed Clean Indoor Air Act gathered in the Capitol rotunda in Harrisburg, Pennsylvania, to give the bill their approval. Dr. J. Edwin Wood of the American Heart Association speaks while cigarettes burn in an ashtray to his left. Listed behind them are the harmful chemicals found in cigarettes.

> "If they haven't figured out how to get rid of the stuff after thirty years, they ought to shut the plants down. It's like building an eating place without a garbage disposal."
>
> Albert Coleman, Jr., environmentalist, on nuclear waste disposal

smoking harmed lungs, hearts, and the newborn, but addiction to the nicotine in tobacco products made quitting difficult. Production in 1990 leveled off to about 75 percent of record 1975 levels, primarily due to aggressive exporting by major American tobacco companies. Never having admitted that tobacco was harmful, the cigarette makers apparently saw nothing wrong with aggressively selling the crop overseas.

One federal agency, the Department of Agriculture, propped up tobacco farmers with price supports while another, Health and Human Services, issued warnings of tobacco's potentially lethal effects. By 1987, as the result of a national antismoking campaign, a federal ruling restricted smoking by 890,000 government employees in sixty-eight hundred federal buildings. Forty states had by this time regulated smoking in varying degrees in public places. No wonder smokers crowded doctors' offices for a prescribed nicotine patch that, when applied to the skin, helped wean them from their addiction.

Yet another worry that carried over from the 1970s and earlier was the fear of radiation contamination. The worst commercial nuclear accident in U.S. history had taken place in 1979 at Three Mile Island, Pennsylvania, and reminders of the dangers of this energy source kept popping up. Workers were accidentally contaminated in Tennessee in 1981, in New York in 1982, and in Oklahoma in 1986. That same year, massive contamination occurred in northeastern Europe as the Soviet Union's Chernobyl nuclear power plant spewed clouds of radiation across parts of several countries. Americans read of the dead and dying of Chernobyl and seemed a bit more inclined to try radical measures to prevent future nuclear energy mishaps.

Times Beach, Love Canal

The EPA, though barely active under Ronald Reagan, nevertheless spent big money in Missouri. Soil in Times Beach, with just twenty-four hundred inhabitants, was discovered in the 1970s to have perilous levels of the toxic chemical, dioxin. EPA Administrator Anne Burford announced early in 1983 that $33 million from her superfund would be used to relocate residents. More than one part per billion was considered hazardous, and Times Beach tests found levels of one hundred parts per billion or more. A cleanup program began once all residents had moved from the tiny town just west of St. Louis.

Somewhat less widespread than Times Beach, but equally frightening, were events surrounding the picturesquely named Love Canal. The body of water was an enlarged ditch in a Niagara Falls, New York, neighborhood. Residents of modest ranch houses in the area learned in the late 1970s that the Hooker Chemical Company, between 1942 and 1953, had dumped an astonishing twenty-one thousand tons of chemical waste in and around the canal. There was more dioxin in Love Canal than had been used in all of Vietnam as the dreaded defoliant, Agent Orange.

Love Canal residents protested, despite the fact that the mayor told them they were creating "bad publicity" for the city. In 1982 and 1983, the state of New York purchased a total of

789 houses in the area, then demolished many of them along with a grammar school. Tons of sod, clay, and plastic were dumped in the "Canal Site Containment Area," which measured three thousand feet long, as much as one hundred feet wide, and up to forty feet deep. After the water and surrounding sites were covered and fenced, plans were put into action to sell existing houses and build new ones at a safe distance.

And Yet More Disasters

Disasters took new and strange shapes, killing huge numbers of people. The worst single-plane disaster in history occurred in Japan in 1985, as a Boeing 747 crashed into a mountainside, killing all 520 passengers and crew. In 1987, Hurricane Hugo killed more than five hundred Americans and Caribbean-island residents during the summer's final week. Television showed the horrors of a massive chemical leak at a Union Carbide plant in Bhopal, India, that killed twenty-three hundred and injured or permanently disabled two hundred thousand others on the night of December 3, 1984. Bhopal was the worst industrial accident in human history.

The immense tragedy in India brought up other troubling questions. Was the lure of foreign investment more important to emerging countries than human safety or the environment? Would the $3 billion suit brought against Union Carbide result in the loss of American jobs and the disappearance of stockholders' investments? Who was morally responsible for the hundreds of Indians blinded by the chemical leak? Obviously, there was a serious downside to multinational business.

An Earthquake and a Volcanic Eruption

TV delivered — in a coincidental way — the decade's most widely witnessed disaster on October 17, 1989. Millions of Americans awaited the start of a World Series baseball game, set for Candlestick Park in San Francisco, when ABC-TV's network transmission was snapped by a powerful earthquake. Viewers learned that the game would be cancelled and that greater San Francisco had been jolted by a quake measuring 6.9 on the Richter scale. A total of sixty-six

Weeds grow around boarded up homes in the Love Canal area in June 1980 Hooker Chemicals had dumped toxic waste there over an eleven-year period from 1942 and 1953. In the late seventies and early eighties, the area was evacuated and most of the homes were demolished.

people died in and after the rumble, which lasted just a few seconds, but managed to collapse freeways, crumble buildings, and start fires. The San Francisco Bay-area quake caught thousands of commuters on their way home from work with no warning whatsoever.

Hundreds of miles up the coast and years earlier, in 1980, Mount Saint Helens had blown its top. More accurately, the state of Washington's long-dormant volcano blew out its mountainous side, resulting in sixty deaths and damage that totaled an estimated $3 billion. The force of the eruption was five hundred times that of the atomic bomb dropped on Hiroshima during World War II. Unlike the unsuspecting Japanese in 1945, residents and sightseers were warned in advance of the potential for disaster. Many of those who died were people who chose to stay put. They died in their homes and in their cars as ash choked off oxygen and burned vegetation. The material from the eruption affected the world's weather for some time afterwards.

Artificial Disasters

Other forms of life died as a result of disasters caused by humans. The largest oil spill in U.S. history took place in 1989 in Alaska's Prince William Sound. Some eleven million gallons of crude oil leaked out of the *Exxon Valdez* after the ship ran aground on March 24. Exxon told the public that it accepted full responsibility for the catastrophe, but in a few days it became clear that no one could fully contain the slick, which stretched for forty-five miles along a previously unspoiled shoreline. Fish, birds, and other animals perished, commercial fisheries lost money, and Alaskans asked if the pipeline bringing oil from vast reserves on their North Slope was worth the trouble.

A car is buried in rubble from collapsed stores on Pacific Avenue, Santa Cruz, after a huge earthquake hit the San Francisco area on October 17, 1989. Casualties were severe because many commuters were on the roads as the quake struck.

As equipment aged, new kinds of scares swept the land. Aloha Airlines Flight 243 lost a huge chunk of its fourteen-year-old fuselage on April 29, 1988, some hundred miles away from and twenty-four thousand feet above Honolulu. A stewardess was sucked out of the plane and never found, but

dying were tangled in the wreckage, which was traced to faulty construction in a portion of the modern building. In contrast to the graphic photos of twisted metal and collapsed concrete, few people outside the military or the Rockwell Corporation saw any direct evidence in 1984 when

the passengers, battered by incredible turbulence, all survived. Sixty of the ninety-five persons aboard were injured, despite a safe landing on the island of Maui. A probe of the freakish mishap reported that years of exposure to salt air may have weakened the airliner's aluminum body.

And, in what may have been the most senseless and frightening mishap of all, partygoers at a Hyatt Regency Hotel in Kansas City, Missouri, were killed in 1981 when a huge walkway collapsed. A total of 111 dead and

the country's top-secret B-1 bomber crashed in the California desert during a test flight.

Americans responded to all such events in predictable ways. The religious became more so, resigned to the facts that illnesses, deaths, and accidents were God's will. The nonreligious turned to everything from self-help support groups to alcohol and other drugs, and those in between tried to forget about how easily, frequently, and swiftly sickness and tragedy could strike.

A clean-up operation takes place on Smith Island, Alaska, after the massive oil spill in Prince William Sound in March 1989. Water from a perforated hose pours sea water over the stones to wash the oil into the sea. Despite all efforts, the formerly pristine environment of the Alaskan shoreline was polluted by oil along a forty-five-mile stretch.

CHAPTER 4
A Freer Hand for Corporations

There was a gulp of apple juice left and the young mother quickly swallowed it before putting her baby's cup into the rack and closing the dishwasher. She hit the button and heard the appliance hum before the taste in her mouth — or lack of it — stopped her in her tracks. She called a friend.

"Judy, the next time you're here I want you to taste this Beech-Nut apple juice," the mother said, eyeing the container suspiciously. "I know apple juice doesn't have a strong flavor, but the stuff I just drank tastes like water with nothing but sugar in it. Either my taste buds are gone or this stuff never came near an apple. It's just colored water!"

The young woman asked others to sample the juice, and they confirmed her thoughts. Afterward, network news reported that two Beech-Nut executives were being tried for having marketed sugary, tinted water as apple juice. Was this an isolated occurrence or a hint of how things were being done?

The Reagan administration may have dropped a hint on January 8, 1982, less than a year after the president took office. The U.S. Justice Department announced that a thirteen-year-old antitrust suit against International Business Machines Corp (IBM) would be dropped. The legal action was "without merit," the government admitting that its actions in the case were "flimsy."

The case originated in 1969, with the Justice Department accusing IBM of monopolizing the computer market.

Various judicial matters generated sixty-six million pages of documents and cost the government as much as $13.4 million. Attempts to settle the case failed before federal authorities finally agreed with IBM that the market had changed enormously. The decision was seen as an instance of common sense rather than the Reagan administration rolling over and playing dead for big business.

"Dead" was the best way to describe other makers of home computers that failed to keep pace technologically. Once-familiar computer names such as Commodore, Franklin, Leading Edge, and Texas Instruments left the market in the 1980s as IBM and Apple increased their influence, though their share of home-computer sales actually dropped amid a flood of PCs from the Far East.

The Breakup of AT&T

In more momentous news, the American Telephone & Telegraph Company on January 1, 1984, divested itself of its twenty-two Bell System local phone companies. The breakup took place after the U.S. Supreme Court upheld the decision to dissolve the huge conglomerate, a decision based on antitrust laws intended to prevent monopolies.

AT&T continued to offer long-distance telephone service. It was joined by major rivals such as MCI and

Donald Trump.

No one better symbolized the tasteless excess of the 1980s than Donald Trump. A shameless self-promoter, Trump was the son of well-to-do New York parents. He took the sizeable sum of money made by his father in real estate and built an empire worth millions by making big deals.

Trump seemed to excel at two things: getting his face on the covers of magazines and buying huge buildings, most of them in Manhattan. At the height of his power, he owned Trump Tower, a Fifth Avenue, New York, condominium; Trump Castle, an Atlantic City gambling casino; the Trump Shuttle, an airline running between Boston, New York City, and Washington, D.C.; a 47-room "cottage" in Connecticut; and a 117-room mansion in Palm Beach, Florida.

Trump preferred traveling by helicopter, so he purchased a French Puma. The Puma featured bulletproof glass, everything from leather seats to missile-launching capability, and the name "Trump" splashed in huge red letters on either side. He also owned a gold-trimmed, $30 million yacht four stories high with an elevator and filled with paintings by Old Masters. Trump's bedroom on board the craft included a shower made of a single piece of carved marble. Despite his excesses, Americans were almost saddened when Trump fell on hard times.

Like many other high rollers, he was financially wounded in 1989 when the junk-bond market collapsed. Bankers and others wanted money he owed and they forced him to sell off some of his holdings.

At the top of his career, Trump had hired a ghostwriter to produce a book he titled *The Art of the Deal*. Because Americans have always had a fascination with wealth, the book sold like crazy. After his empire hit the skids, he conceived another book called *Trump: Surviving at the Top*.

Historians will point to Donald Trump — and to others, such as Wall Street's Henry Kravis and newspaper mogul Rupert Murdoch — as symbols of the greed of the decade.

Sprint and by numerous regional long-distance carriers. Special incentives were offered to consumers and businesses alike. As the decade ended, approximately 70 percent of phone customers were still AT&T long-distance subscribers.

AT&T gained ground in other areas. It was allowed to keep major subsidiaries such as Bell Laboratories, where dozens of important inventions had been created over the years. Even more important, the Federal Communications Commission allowed the huge corporation into the unregulated field of computer equipment and data-processing services. No doubt this made IBM and all other hardware and software companies quake, since AT&T was already all over the map, in possession of an electronic network like no other corporation on earth.

The numbers attached to the breakup agreement were staggering.

The twenty-two Bell System local operating units were worth $80 billion, or about two-thirds of AT&T's total assets. The Justice Department estimated that it had spent $15 million prosecuting the case, while AT&T spent about $360 million in its defense. The breakup was as momentous as actions taken against Standard Oil and the Rockefeller family in the early 1900s.

To the consumer, not a great deal changed. The telephone itself, whether purchased from a Bell company or from the local appliance store, became almost an added limb for many Americans in the 1980s. Phone use was skyrocketing. Facsimile, or fax, technology — the sending of documents over phone lines — made long-distance service even more important to business.

Ted Turner.

Robert Edward (Ted) Turner inherited a billboard company in Atlanta. What he did with that company is one of the most dramatic business and media success stories in history. Along the way, he had a lot of fun.

Born in 1938, Turner received an Ivy League education in the classics at Brown University, then signed on with the billboard firm in 1961 as a salesperson. He served as president of the company from 1963 to 1970, when he bought an inexpensive television station without network affiliation in Atlanta and founded the Turner Broadcasting System, Inc.

A visionary, Turner realized before virtually anyone else that cable television and satellite technology could put his TV station into homes all across the country — without any kind of network association with ABC, CBS, or NBC. He sent the station's signals into the sky, where they rebounded from satellites to the dishes of local cable services and to dish owners.

Even more important, in 1980 he founded a twenty-four-hour, all-news station, CNN. Unlike the networks, which presented news two or three times daily, CNN (for Cable News Network) ran stories as they developed, seven days a week, around the clock. People more interested in news than the fluff of "Today" or "Good Morning, America" got their news via satellite, from Atlanta. CNN frequently scooped the major networks, if for no other reason than their almost constant broadcast from the newsroom.

Turner purchased the Atlanta Braves baseball team and the Atlanta Hawks basketball team. He also founded and broadcast the Goodwill Games, an Olympics-type event, in 1986. An avid sailor, he won the Americas Cup yacht race in 1977 aboard his boat, *Courageous*. He purchased the MGM Library, a huge stock of old Hollywood movies, giving him thousands of hours of programming for cable-hungry fans. He even listened patiently when fans argued that it would be wrong to colorize old black-and-white movies (Turner colorized them anyway).

Saluted at one time or another by everyone from the Veterans of Foreign Wars to the National Association for the Advancement of Colored People, the Atlanta-based entrepreneur came within an eyelash of buying the CBS television network at the close of the decade. Jane Fonda, former activist, fitness expert, and movie star, was his third wife.

Merger Mania

Nine of the ten largest corporate mergers and acquisitions ever took place in the 1980s. The biggest of them all was R. J. Reynolds, the tobacco company, and Nabisco, maker of cookies, crackers, and cereal. The firms were acquired by Kohlberg, Kravis, & Roberts in a leveraged buyout that totaled $24.9 billion. (A leveraged buyout involves rounding up money in order to buy a large company. If enough money is acquired to buy the company, persons who lent the money become shareholders in the newly acquired firm. If the buyout doesn't happen, the money is returned.) Time, Inc. and Warner Brothers merged at a price of $13.9 billion, and Chevron acquired Gulf Oil for $13.3 billion.

Leona Helmsley.

America began the 1980s angry at the poor. By decade's end, they were angry at the rich — or angry at one of the rich, at least. Their ire was focused on Leona Helmsley, called "The Lady Macbeth of the Lodging Industry." What had the second wife of real-estate tycoon Harry Helmsley done?

Born and reared in Brooklyn, Leona added a phony college degree and a nonexistent modeling career to her resume, eventually becoming a successful apartment broker in Manhattan. She engineered a meeting with Helmsley and was impressive enough so that the wheeler-dealer left his wife of thirty-three years to marry Leona in 1972.

As Harry became older and more feeble, Leona took control. Her husband was worth at least $5 billion, and she ran his chain of hotels as if every cent mattered. Business expenses on the couple's tax return included a $130,000 stereo system for their twenty-eight-room mansion, artwork worth more than $500,000, a cruise charter costing $28,500, and many thousands more in clothes, cosmetics, beauty services, and hairdressing.

She never seemed to tire of putting down the help. Painting contractors she hired to repaint her mansion were not permitted to use any of the bathrooms — even when they were painting a bathroom! She put her face on thirty-six of the fifty-two post-cards available at Helmsley hotels, and she snarled at waiters and waitresses trying to please her.

Harry was a crook, too, but he got off because he was senile. No one was willing to cut Leona any slack, least of all the many employees she terrorized before seeing to it that they were fired. "I don't pay taxes," she once thundered to an employee. "Only the little people pay taxes!"

Mrs. Helmsley went on trial for tax evasion in the summer of 1989 with a brilliant defense. Her attorney told the jury that, of course, the woman was "a bitch," but that should not result in her being found guilty. The prosecution proved to the jurors that Leona's paper trail of phony invoices amounted to intent to evade paying what she owed. The jury found her guilty and she was sentenced to four years in prison, 750 hours of community service, and $7.1 million in fines.

Michael Milken.

There was nothing in Michael Milken's background to suggest how he would end up. From a prosperous, middle-class family living in Encino, California, Milken was a good student and a cheerleader in high school. He attended the University of California at Berkeley and studied hard during a time when many other college kids were taking drugs and protesting the Vietnam War.

Milken married his high school sweetheart and moved east to Philadelphia to attend graduate school in business. He read voraciously and after earning an advanced degree, joined a small investment banking firm that would become Drexel Burnham Lambert. Milken soon was dealing in low-rated and unrated securities, investments that were said to be risky but that paid potentially large dividends. He made a fortune.

The young man opened an office in Beverly Hills, working from 4:30 A.M. till late into the evening each day. He took huge fees for his services, plus large percentages of the income that normally would have gone to his employer, Drexel. By the late 1970s, the utterly humorless, frequently snappish Milken was a millionaire several times over.

The more he made, the more he wanted. Ivan F. Boesky in 1986 told federal investigators that Milken was one of many persons who had benefited from advanced insider trading knowledge. Milken denied ninety-eight charges the government brought against him, hiring expensive attorneys and even a public relations firm to improve his image. The lawyers and the publicity makers battered the government while portraying Milken as a man with an expansive social conscience.

Eventually, Milken pleaded guilty to six felonies and was fined $600 million — only a small percentage of the money he had manipulated. Drexel was fined $650 million. Milken agreed to plead guilty to filing false statements, securities fraud, mail fraud, filing false tax returns, and more. Perhaps because he felt he could not endure the humiliation of a trial, he admitted wrongdoing. Milken was sentenced to ten years in prison by Judge Kimba Wood, who demolished his defense before handing down five consecutive two-year sentences.

MEXICAN & AMERICAN

Groups holding large shares of stock lined up on different sides in the acquisition tug of war. They were forced to do so because "mergers and acquisitions" departments of investment–banking firms were playing both sides of the fence in a competition with huge amounts of money at stake. Some of the department would help an outsider take over a firm, while others would help that firm fend off the takeover. The entire matter was done by buying or selling the company's stock. Shareholders were offered generous sums if they would turn over their shares in the company to whomever was trying to accomplish the takeover. The company in danger of takeover and its allies would buy up the stock to prevent a takeover.

This manipulation had huge consequences. Companies forced to fend off takeovers often were left with little or no cash for research and development or for expansion. Companies that were successfully taken over by outsiders often found they had been purchased so that the outsiders could make money by liquidating them. Often this was done solely to eliminate competition. Thousands of workers lost jobs during such goings-on. By the end of the decade, there were many Americans over the age of fifty who had been cut loose from careers with companies they once thought secure, never to find good jobs again.

The takeovers were financed by the sale of so-called junk bonds. Bonds would be issued by a person who urged people to buy them so that he could get enough money (or "leverage") to take over the stock of a company he had in mind. If he raised enough money, the people who bought his junk bonds were handsomely rewarded — often from the profits made by selling off pieces of the company taken over. Michael Milken and others were geniuses at creating and selling such pieces of paper. There was nothing illegal in these games when played by the rules. In fact, media mogul Ted Turner almost gained control of the CBS television network by issuing junk bonds.

Unfortunately, some of the most successful merger and acquisitions people operated outside the law. It has always been illegal to benefit from information not available to the average investor, but financiers like Dennis Levine, Ivan F. Boesky, Martin Siegel, and Michael Milken violated that law and others. They obtained insider information and traded back and forth, so that they could purchase stocks and bonds at a low price and sell them for much more. Levine was arrested in 1986 after making $12.6 million in insider-trading profits. He had paid to find out what companies were about to do financially, making money on such privileged information. He maintained secret bank accounts in Switzerland and in the Caribbean, which did him no good while he served a two-year prison term. Boesky served three years, Siegel only two months, and Milken twenty-two months.

"Black Monday"

The junk-bond market collapsed, but the cause of the collapse was only indirectly related to the creation of such leverage instruments. What caused junk bonds to decline was the stock market. Throughout the 1980s, in good times and in bad, the stock market shot skyward. The Dow Jones Industrial Average, a measure of the market, had climbed from about eleven hundred points to more than twenty-seven hundred in the late summer of 1987. In the first eight months of 1987, the market hit record highs fifty-five times. Several respected economists warned that there were parallels between the 1987 market and the ill-fated market of 1929, but the buying public paid little heed.

The stock market crash of 1987 took place on October 19. It differed from the more famous crash that signaled the beginning of the Great

---

ECONOMY

For further information see primary source entries on pages

11: 1526-28, 1537-39, 1550-53; **12:** 1611-12, 1680-81, 1702-03, 1722-26

The New York Stock Exchange in October 1987. "Black Monday" was the worst day in its history, when six hundred million shares were traded, and $500 billion were wiped off the value of stocks. The chairman of the stock exchange described it as "the nearest thing to a meltdown that I ever want to see."

hand and outpriced by the discount stores on the other. Traditional department stores consolidated as their sales decreased, too. Among all consumer prices, only gasoline failed to climb significantly during the period.

Besides retailing, commercial airlines were finding the 1980s a tough time in which to do business. Deregulation of the industry actually began under Jimmy Carter, but its effects were felt most sharply in the 1980s. Braniff went bankrupt in 1982, started up again in 1984, and went out of business again shortly thereafter. Consoli-

dations caused the symbols of Republic, People's Express, Allegheny, and Piedmont to disappear from tails of planes all across the country. The largest airline in the free world — Eastern — was also the most troubled. Despite trading stock with pilots for cuts in pay and other measures, the airline took on its unionized employees and lost. As the decade ended, Eastern, under Frank Lorenzo, folded its wings. But several upstart airlines, including no-frills Southwest, prospered.

Unlike most airlines, America's automotive industry experienced

American workers produce Subaru cars and Isuzu trucks at a plant in Lafayette, Indiana. Japanese businesses such as Isuzu, Mazda, Mitsubishi, and Honda opened car plants in the Midwest in the 1980s.

somewhat of a resurgence in the 1980s, though there were major changes. Once the largest and flabbiest of U.S. industries, the auto business had been forced to pay attention to the number of Japanese cars being sold domestically. In 1989, the Honda Accord, conceived in Japan and assembled in Ohio, was the nation's most popular car. Two Toyotas and a Nissan model also were among the top ten bestsellers. Because the dollar declined in value compared to the Japanese yen, making imported cars too expensive for the average American, Honda, Toyota, Nissan, and others built assembly plants here, frequently turning to local suppliers to create truly international vehicles. It became more difficult to "Buy American" when Hondas were made in Ohio, Toyotas in Kentucky, and Nissans in Tennessee!

The Big Three U.S. automakers, Chrysler, Ford, and General Motors, were different places to work than they had been a decade earlier. Chrysler, under Lee Iacocca, was competitive once again, after being propped up in the late 1970s by federal money. Ford and General Motors both had joint-venture assembly-lines with the Japanese, Ford working with Toyota on a new line in northern Ohio, and G.M. joining Toyota on the West Coast for production facilities. Ford and G.M. were enjoying brisk pickup truck sales, and Chrysler minivans were being copied by Ford, General Motors, and everyone else. Sales exceeded eleven million vehicles three times in the 1980s.

U.S. machines kept a steady 20 percent of the worldwide market, with the domestic manufacturers in the top ten among all U.S. exporters. The leading exporter was Boeing, having met the booming Asian market — and

the threat of competition from Europe — with such planes as the 757 and the 767. Other leading exporters included General Electric, IBM, McDonnell Douglas, DuPont, Caterpillar, United Technologies, Hewlett-Packard, Philip Morris, Eastman Kodak, and Motorola.

Thanks to better record keeping and faster reporting, Americans became aware that some sections of the country were cheaper places to live than others. During the recession of the early eighties, for example, housing prices fell to half their original value in cities such as Houston. Office-building vacancy rates were sky high in Dallas, leading some companies to relocate, particularly from the East Coast. Houses in states with declining population, such as North Dakota or West Virginia, seldom sold for what they were worth, recession or not. Median housing prices climbed from $66,400 in 1981 to $97,500 in 1990. Migration to Texas and California slowed, but Florida continued to lure northerners, particularly those who were retired.

Agriculture

Farmers, by tradition, vote Republican. They turned out in large numbers to help put Ronald Reagan into office in 1980, to reelect him in 1984, and to elect George Bush in 1988. The trouble was, in each election there were fewer farmers around to cast votes. They might have been even less influential had not the entire country been set up long ago to give rural residents a big say in government.

Republican free-market advocates missed a good chance in the 1980s to detach farmers from federal support. Instead, the Reagan administration

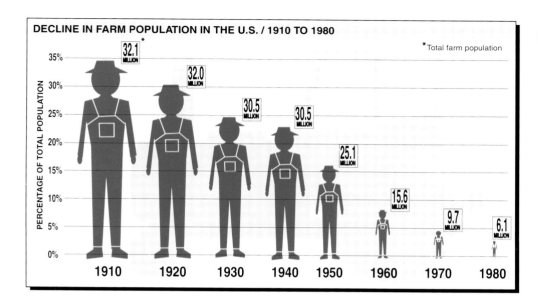

DECLINE IN FARM POPULATION IN THE U.S. / 1910 TO 1980

*Total farm population

1910	32.1 MILLION
1920	32.0 MILLION
1930	30.5 MILLION
1940	30.5 MILLION
1950	25.1 MILLION
1960	15.6 MILLION
1970	9.7 MILLION
1980	6.1 MILLION

(PERCENTAGE OF TOTAL POPULATION axis: 0%, 5%, 10%, 15%, 20%, 25%, 30%, 35%)

Although the number of people in farming remained stable until the 1940s, it was already declining as a percentage of the total population. From then on, the number of people making a living on the land drastically declined. In the seventy years from 1910 to 1980, numbers in farming decreased from over one in three of the total population of the U.S. to just over one in forty.

continued to allow ranchers to cheaply graze their stock on public land and others to receive money when they raised too much of a given crop and prices fell. Nevertheless, public demand affected the business: The number of cattle, for example, dropped from 111,242 in 1980 to 98,162 in 1990, perhaps because physicians were warning about over-consumption of red meat. Corn, wheat, and barley were the most plentiful grain crops, and the U.S. remained the world's leading exporter of wheat and corn. But it was hard to get fair prices for commodities because Europe and Japan heavily subsidized their own farmers. Farm debt declined by 15 percent, but farm income went down, too, to 1970 levels. Average farm size increased during the decade from 427 to 467 acres.

By 1990, just 2.4 percent of all employed Americans had jobs directly connected to farming, but that wasn't entirely because farming was a depressed occupation. Instead, farmers frequently relied on computers programmed by agricultural scientists to tell them when and where to plant and harvest and on techniques such as no-till farming to keep them in business. Machines increasingly did the work of farm hands as sizeable numbers of farmers began to see themselves as managers of a given piece of property. The wholesome, rural, perhaps backward, image of farming harbored by many Americans in the 1980s simply bore little or no relation to reality.

Another phenomenon about which less was heard was corporate farming. Farming in the Midwest in the 1960s and early 1970s looked so prosperous to Chicago bankers that they thought about buying $3,000-per-acre farms in lush, central Illinois and selling shares in the ownership. But such absentee ownership lost its appeal as farm prices declined in the 1980s. That decline was mirrored in the empty storefronts of small towns and the "For Sale" signs that sprouted more readily than many of the crops. By the end of the decade, neither private nor corporate farming was seen as the romantic work it had seemed during America's first two hundred years.

CHAPTER 5
Islam Ascends, Communism Declines

A hijacked TWA airliner at Beirut airport in June 1985. Thirty-nine American hostages were eventually released, but one passenger, Robert Stethem, a navy diver, was murdered. The hijackers declared "America is the great Satan."

The Mercedes truck swung in a clumsy circle around an unguarded parking lot and began slowly to accelerate. It had cleared Lebanese and U.S. Marine checkpoints and now was on an airport access road headed toward marine headquarters, where hundreds of American soldiers slept. The driver gunned his engine, dodging a barbed-wire fence, and swerved between two sentry posts, his truck filled with TNT. The vehicle smashed into the lobby of the Americans' building before the explosives

were detonated. It was 6:22 A.M. on October 23, 1983, in Beirut.

Some 241 U.S. Marines and U.S. Navy personnel died in the blast. Less than two minutes later, fifty French paratroopers nearby were killed in the same sort of truck-bomb attack. Guerrilla groups allied with Iran or Syria were blamed for the carnage, which resulted in more single-day casualties than the marines experienced at any time in the Vietnam War. Like so many well-meaning ventures involving Americans as

peacekeepers, the foray into Beirut had disastrous results.

If sending Americans to separate warring foreigners lost some of its appeal in the 1980s, the appeal of Islam among its followers was never stronger. Conservative religious leaders, buoyed by the Islamic revolution in Iran in 1979, pressured their own political leaders and foreigners alike. Egypt suffered immense, daily turmoil, with battles between Muslims and Christians forcing martial law in September 1981. A few weeks later, President Anwar el-Sadat was assassinated. From the Philippines to Algeria, fundamentalists attacked symbols of Western culture, forming political and guerrilla groups that sometimes served as religious armies.

Nowhere was Islamic attention more focused than in Afghanistan. There, the Soviet Union had moved in to prop up an unpopular Communist puppet. Islamic leaders urged their followers to wage a holy war against the forces of godless communism, and young and old Muslims from all across the world migrated to the Afghan mountains to kill Soviet soldiers. The United Nations arranged a cease-fire in 1988, after almost a decade of fighting in which fifteen thousand Soviet troops died. Though most Soviet units withdrew from Afghanistan, extremist Muslim rebels continued the fighting, sometimes among themselves.

America's awareness of Islam was increasing for many reasons. First, there were nearly eight million Muslims in America, making them one of the fastest growing religious groups. Second, Arabs, Palestinians, and other mostly Islamic Middle Eastern people viewed America's long-standing commitment to Israel as an insult and were getting more vocal. Third, U.S. military alliances with leaders in Saudi Arabia, Jordan, and elsewhere made these leaders suspect among fundamental followers of the Islamic religion, and the resulting unrest made international news. Finally, Islam's treatment of women as inferior to men incensed progressive U.S. women, who were already angry at the conservative Reagan administration for its opposition to such things as abortion and the Equal Rights Amendment.

Terrorism

The wild card in all this was terrorism. Hundreds of Muslims and Muslim sympathizers carried on a war of terror during the decade, taking on the superior armaments of Israel, Europe, and the United States. Many of the terrorist attacks were in response to military measures taken by Israel or its allies. In 1981, for example, a worried Israel bombed an Iraqi nuclear reactor, despite earlier claims by Saddam Hussein that the facility was under construction for peaceful purposes. Israeli intelligence had paid a French worker at the facility to hide a homing device inside the building. When Israeli jets attacked, they simply flew toward the electronic signal.

There followed many bombings, kidnappings, and related terrorist activities, making it impossible to directly connect an action by Israelis or Americans with a reaction by terrorists. Americans shot down two Libyan planes over a body of water claimed by Libya as its own but identified by the U.S. as international water. Early the next year, 1982, U.S. General James Dozier was kidnapped in Italy. Though Italian Communists pulled off the kidnapping, they may have been in sympathy with Libya or Iraq or anyone at odds with the United States.

In 1983, terrorists blew up the U.S. embassy in Beirut, Lebanon, once a resort city on the eastern end of the Mediterranean that has been fought over and reduced to rubble in recent years. More than one hundred

The horror of this decade-long confrontation can be summarized in two events. The first took place in 1982 in Lebanon. Warring Christian Lebanese leader Bashir Gemayel was mysteriously assassinated. A few days later, in two Beirut refugee camps apparently run by the Israelis, Christian militiamen gunned down six hun-

On October 23, 1983, the U.S. Marines' headquarters in Beirut was completely destroyed by Muslim terrorists who drove a truck containing twenty-five hundred pounds of TNT into the building; 241 U.S. personnel died in the blast.

people, most of them American, died in the blast. A few months later, the truck bomb took its toll on the U.S. Marine base. Palestinian terrorists in 1985 seized a Mediterranean cruise ship, the *Achille Lauro*, and killed a wheelchair-bound American. A short while later, Arab terrorists killed a total of twenty people in attacks at the Rome and Vienna airports. There were additional terrorist activities in other European countries.

dred Palestinians. Six years later and thousands of miles away, a terrorist bomb aboard a Pan Am jet headed for the United States killed 280 people. The massacre in Beirut and the air disaster over Lockerbie, Scotland, had only one common denominator — innocent, uninvolved people became the victims.

The line between terrorism and government acts could be thin. Iraq attacked its Kurdish minority with

War II. The only positive thing about communism was that it had kept warring ethnic groups from each other's throats for many years, though it only did so by using the weapons of fear.

NATO Allies Disagree

Like the Soviet Union, the United States was being pressured by its allies during the 1980s. France and West Germany in particular were more eager to talk peace with the Soviet Union than was the United States. Despite both being members of the defensive force known as the North Atlantic Treaty Organization (NATO), America and Germany disagreed over relations with Communist states. Consequently, Germany forged early economic agreements with the Soviets that bothered the Reagan administration. On the opposite side of the globe, Japan refused to contribute much toward anticommunist defense, preferring instead to build up a huge monetary surplus selling cars, electronic goods, and appliances abroad to anyone who could afford them. Only Great Britain under Margaret Thatcher consistently backed Reagan's cautious approach to improving East-West relations.

The disintegration of European communism had almost as important an effect on the United States as on Europe itself. Suddenly, there was no enemy. The Soviet Union, feared by some Americans as a mighty and mysterious military machine, turned out to be a huge country overrun by poor people with terrible — but not terribly reliable — weapons. Suddenly, the sprawling defense plants in California and elsewhere appeared almost pointless. Why make antimissile mis-siles if no one was aiming a missile your way? If the transition from communism to democracy jolted Europe, it rocked the U.S. as well.

Grenada and Panama

In nearby Grenada and Panama, America was directly involved. Grenada is a tiny island of about eighty thousand people, about a hundred miles north of the coast of Venezuela. Left-wing members of the country's military imprisoned its prime minister, Maurice Bishop, before he was freed, rearrested, and then executed. The

In this January 1990 picture, a heavy smog lies over the East German city of Leipzig. The entire former Eastern Bloc was suffering from outdated industrial technology and pollution on a terrifying scale. Western money and expertise would be needed to attempt a cleanup.

Reagan administration acted quickly after learning that Grenada was accepting aid in the form of military advisors from Cuba. U.S. forces, with the assistance of half a dozen of Grenada's neighbors, invaded the island on October 25, 1983. Cuban and Grenadan military personnel were quickly subdued, and the Americans were welcomed by much of the population.

Democrats nor anyone else pointed out that the secret invasion was a violation of the Constitution, since only Congress has the right to make war. Was this a war? Conservatives in particular hailed it as a victory, and no one seemed to mind that the news media was told little or nothing.

Six years later and a thousand miles to the west, American troops

A demonstration in Philadelphia to protest deployment of cruise missiles in Europe. During the 1980s, improving East-West relations led many people to realize the opportunity to end old Cold War antagonisms and cooperate economically with the Soviets.

Ronald Reagan had given no indication to Congress, the press, or the public that he was contemplating an invasion of Grenada. Since the head of state had been killed, no official had pleaded with Reagan to send troops. The president mentioned only on the morning of the invasion that some decisions he had made in his two years in office were most difficult. Perhaps because he was so popular with American voters, neither

invaded Panama at the behest of President George Bush. Unlike Grenada, the U.S. had, for almost a century, been deeply involved in the politics of this Central American nation. This time, politics was entwined with the South American drug trade; Panamanian dictator Manuel Noriega apparently allowed drug smugglers to use his country of 2.5 million people as a stopover on the way north to the United States. Grand juries in the

U.S. accused Noriega of drug involvement shortly before American forces stormed into his country on December 20, 1989.

The fighting was brief but sometimes intense and involved air power. Several Panamanian civilians were killed. Noriega eventually sought refuge with foreign diplomats — he called the Vatican mission from a Dairy Queen to ask for asylum! The dictator surrendered ten days later and was flown to the United States. Convicted of eight counts of racketeering and drug trafficking in the U.S. District Court in Miami in 1992, Noriega remained in a Florida prison.

Numerous countries made front-page headlines, only to be shoved aside by more recent events. Typical was a World War II ally and American friend, the Philippines. The western Pacific island country deposed Ferdinand Marcos and his big-spending wife, Imelda, in 1986, following an election marked by wholesale fraud. Mrs. Marcos left behind hundreds of pairs of shoes, all the while denying her extravagance. The Marcos family settled in New York, then Hawaii, where the elderly dictator died. His legally elected successor, President Corazon Aquino, was beset by economic woes, antigovernment guerrillas, and an untrustworthy military. The country made headlines here late in the decade when it was given back the U.S. naval base at Subic Bay, near Manila.

Looking back over events, the fall of communism was no guarantee of world peace. In fact, it set the stage for deadly struggles among ethnic groups in places such as Yugoslavia. Even more frightening, the former Soviets were willing to sell weapons to the highest bidder. Technology was peddled, too, sometimes by scientists who were suddenly without their Soviet salaries. The breakup of the Soviet Union was counterbalanced by the growing number of countries, many of them badly governed, with nuclear and other dangerous weapons at their disposal.

U.S. soldiers in Panama City. In December 1989, after several years of deteriorating relations between the U.S. and Panama in which the U.S. had tried to end the brutal Noriega regime, Panama declared that a state of war existed between the two countries. Three days later, Bush ordered a successful invasion of Panama to capture Noriega and to help set up a democratic government.

CHAPTER 6
Popular Culture's Strange Celebrities

Michael Jackson's first solo album was "Off the Wall" in 1979. He became one of the rock superstars of the 1980s, winning Grammy Awards and selling millions of albums and videos.

How strange were the 1980s? Before Pepsi-Cola signed a contract with Michael Jackson, no one would have guessed that a hugely successful advertiser would put millions of marketing dollars behind a skinny young man who looked and acted like a girl, who had undergone cosmetic surgery, and who attracted attention by walking backwards as he sang.

Jackson had started humbly enough. The youngest of five singing sons of a Gary, Indiana, couple, Michael joined his brothers to sing and dance as soon as he was old enough to talk. The group, known as The Jackson Five, signed a contract with Motown Records in Detroit and had a string of hits in the early 1970s. Little was heard of Michael during his teen years, but he returned with a dazzling solo act in 1983. A single, "Beat It," and the album on which it was released, "Thriller," earned Grammy Awards that year. Jackson's frantic and controversial dancing, which proved that the feet could be quicker than the eye, was attempted with varying degrees of success by preteen kids. Kids in the mid-1980s "moonwalked" backwards to and from schools all across the country.

When kids weren't imitating Michael Jackson, they were break dancing. Conceived in black urban neighborhoods, the moves involved writhing joints, swooping leaps, and sudden drops and spins to the pavement or floor. For full effect, a disc jockey forced records accompanying the dance to stop, spin backwards, and emit rhythmic, scratchy noises. A rapper or poet often delivered tight, tough rhymes that, when taken together, resulted in rap music. Break dancing became hip-hop, while rap lyrics gained incredible popularity

among black and white high school students and younger listeners, most of them male.

The Material Girl

Equally bizarre was Madonna, who admitted as no entertainer ever has that she was a material girl — she loved money. But she loved to be outrageous even more. . . .

Born Madonna Ciccone in suburban Detroit, this daughter of a middle-class, Roman Catholic couple trained as a dancer, then spent a year at the University of Michigan before heading to New York City to seek her fortune. She worked in at least one X-rated film while trying to make it as a singer, a line of work that eventually resulted in her first hit single, an album, and her introduction to fame as the star of an MTV video.

Madonna's songs and her actions showed that she had few illusions. She urged her female listeners to act "Like a Virgin," admitting that she was willing to be a "boy toy" (a sexual object)

Madonna trained as a dancer before turning to singing. Her album, "Madonna" (1983), included five hit singles. Since then, she has starred in several films and a Broadway play, and given a number of worldwide concert tours.

"We are living in a material world and I am a material girl."

Madonna

if rewards were sure to follow. Such messages weren't any more outrageous than most of the other videos and records at the time, and Madonna recruited millions of young listeners. Many of them were girls in their early teens who became Madonna "wannabees" by dressing and acting like the entertainer. Her costumes often had big safety pins and a patched together look. She filled stadiums and concert halls by singing and dancing in costumes that revealed her increasingly sculptured form.

Madonna soon attracted the attention of Hollywood. She starred in several movies, including *Who's That Girl? Desperately Seeking Susan,* and *Dick Tracy.* Not many could be considered box-office successes. She returned to New York City in triumph, acting in a David Mamet play entitled *Speed the Plow.*

Her worldwide concert tours continued to sell out, though a huge segment of the population paid her little heed, and a few actively protested the fact that she acted in a sexual way while wearing a cross on a string around her neck.

Changing Musical Tastes

Most Americans had grown up with rock music. Pop, for all its dazzle, couldn't compare to rock 'n' roll in the eyes of the over-thirty crowd. With time to listen and money to spend on the new compact discs and their crisp-sounding CD players, listeners went in two directions: They supported a few very talented rockers, such as Eric Clapton, John Mellencamp, Bruce Springsteen, and Tina Turner; and they turned in droves to radio stations that played the oldies of

their youth. Sixties rock 'n' roll continued to exert a tremendous influence on rock in the eighties, though sales and airwaves were seriously challenged for the first time by country music.

Country music fans had existed quietly in large numbers for years, not buying many records or tapes but listening steadfastly to favored stations and following the careers of numerous performers. They appeared in droves at county fairs to hear music that was largely shut off the airwaves — until marketing people realized country might sell. Outlaw music, performed by Willie Nelson, Waylon Jennings, and others, sold very well in the 1970s, pulling some fans away from rock. The stage was set for a new generation of performers, heard increasingly on urban FM radio. Called "hat acts" because they usually wore huge, almost comical, cowboy hats, Garth Brooks and George Strait, and women such as Reba McEntire and Emmylou Harris, wooed and won large audiences and appeared with increasing frequency on network prime-time television.

Rock 'n' roll at the start of the decade had become, as an ad later said, "boring and corporate." High school kids and young adults turned to New Wave music, which could be shrill or strange or sad, but was never apt to put the listener to sleep. Groups such as Blondie, Talking Heads, and the Boomtown Rats, among many others, sold briskly to people with attitudes who claimed to really know music. They were joined at the retail outlets by "metal heads" intent on groups such as Bon Jovi or Guns and Roses, and by African-American adult listeners tuning in to noncommercial talent such as Al Green.

Bruce Springsteen.

It was Bruce Springsteen's bad luck that the rockin'est song he ever performed was misinterpreted. "Born in the U.S.A.," which he wrote in 1984, was seen by many fans as a chauvinistic declaration rather than the blue-collar cry for help that Springsteen had intended. Happily, nothing else has gone wrong with his career.

Born in Freehold, New Jersey, in 1949, "The Boss" performed for years in New York and New Jersey nightclubs before earning enough attention to get a recording contract. His first record album, "Greetings From Asbury Park, New Jersey" in 1973, was followed by a nationwide concert tour with the E Street Band.

Springsteen wowed concertgoers with the sheer energy he put into his guitar playing and singing. A string of hit albums followed, including: "Born to Run," 1975; "Born in the U.S.A.," 1984; and "Tunnel of Love," 1987. In addition to gold records, he won Best Pop/Rock Album of the Year in the Downbeat Record Poll of 1984.

Springsteen wrote many of his biggest hits, from "Pink Cadillac" to "Hungry Heart." Unlike many purveyors of rock 'n' roll, he sang songs of impending defeat, wavering confidence, frustration, even failure. Adults picked up on his music long before kids, perhaps because they sensed original messages unlike the predictable, brash lyrics of most of the other rock hits.

Springsteen briefly married actress Julianne Phillips before settling in with Patty Scialfa, one of his backup singers. In a decade marked by the rise of country among older listeners and the rise of New Wave, pop, and rap among the young, The Boss was a reminder that rock 'n' roll still had a lot of life.

At the Movies

Fed by the success of the video-cassette recorder, or VCR, the motion picture business prospered throughout the 1980s. Of the fifty most successful movies of all time, more than half were produced during the decade. They shouldered aside earlier classics and gauged the taste of the nation — and the world. More recent films had the advantage of higher ticket prices, while older movies continued to win new audiences by being reissued or by being available on videotape. By 1990,

Blockbuster Video was a nationwide rental and sales franchise requiring more than $350,000 in start-up costs per outlet. It competed with individual stores in cities and towns all across the country.

The most popular movie of all time until *Jurassic Park*, Steven Spielberg's *E.T., The Extra-Terrestrial*, came out in 1982. Recent figures indicate that $228.6 million was spent on tickets to see the small alien with the appetite for candy, who merely wanted to "phone home." Some of the most popular movies in history were released in the 1980s. They

Steven Spielberg's film E.T., The Extra-Terrestrial is a fantasy about a boy who makes friends with an alien from space, created by Carlo Rambaldi. The film won Oscars for best picture, best original score, and best sound.

include George Lucas's *Return of the Jedi* (1983) and *The Empire Strikes Back* (1980), *Batman* (1989), *Ghostbusters* (1984), and two more Spielberg efforts, *Raiders of the Lost Ark* (1981) and *Indiana Jones and the Last Crusade* (1989).

Several things can be said of these and other modern-day motion pictures: As cable and network television offered a wider variety of viewing possibilities, the movies kept pace by correctly guessing what the American public wanted to see. And, during a period when U.S. goods did not sell well abroad, movies were a dramatic exception, capturing huge audiences in Europe and Asia.

The big winners on the big screen were heavy on action but light on gore, intense violence, or complex plots. Most films were ninety minutes of dazzle built around a sight gag or a plot device that could be shown in five minutes or less.

Were there still big audiences for "serious" movies? Yes. Actors such as Robert DeNiro and Ben Kingsley gave stunning performances, as a boxer in *Raging Bull* and as Mohandas Gandhi in *Gandhi*, respectively, early in the decade.

The period ended with upstart Jodie Foster in *The Accused* and veteran actress Jessica Tandy in *Driving Miss Daisy*, both equally riveting. All four

received Oscars for their performances.

While African-Americans and other minorities were seen routinely on the screen, minorities were scarce in positions of power or authority in entertainment. An exception was Spike Lee, who began in the mid-1980s to produce low-budget films such as *She's Gotta Have It* and *Do the Right Thing*. Lee, a young New Yorker of incredible intensity, examined sex, race relations, interracial love, and other themes that initially scared

off the major studios. He succeeded by teaching blacks about themselves and by revealing to whites the details of life in black America.

What's on TV?

If African-Americans were scarce in positions of power in the movies, they were everywhere on television. No one was more successful, behind or in front of the camera, than Bill

Bill Cosby.

Bill Cosby was at least as recognizable as President Ronald Reagan in the 1980s and probably even better liked. Besides playing the dad in television's top-rated program, he was the most sought-after endorser of products in the country. Coca-Cola, Jell-O, Kodak film — Cosby peddled them all and more.

The entertainer was born in Philadelphia in 1937, and after college became a standup comedian, creating laughs by making up stories about his old neighborhood friends. He became the first African-American man to star in a network television series when he and Robert Culp teamed up as tennis-playing sleuths from 1965 to 1968 in "I Spy." The comedian, who found the time to earn a doctorate degree in education, has been in the spotlight ever since.

Bill Cosby with Barbara Bush (left) and Dr. Dorothy I. Height, president of the National Council of Negro Women.

Kids got to know "Cos" well, since he made guest appearances on everything from public television's "The Electric Company" to "Captain Kangaroo." A youthful, cartoon Cosby and neighborhood chums, such as Fat Albert, showed up for several years in a series on Saturday-morning television. The entertainer did the voices of the whole cast.

But it was his prime-time comedy, "The Bill Cosby Show," that made him a household name. The thirty-minute weekly show on Thursday evenings depicted an upper-middle-class black family living in New York City. Though criticized for showing too fanciful a picture of African-Americans at a time when their lot was a hard one, the series was a spectacular success from its debut in 1984.

The show spawned a number of Hollywood films, most of them comedies. They crowded Cosby's credentials, which already included four television Emmy awards and a recording-industry Grammy. While setting concert attendance records at places such as Radio City music hall in New York City in 1986, Cosby also managed to pen several books, most of them lighthearted pieces of advice. Titles include *Fatherhood* (1986) and *Love and Marriage* (1989). Immensely wealthy, he and his wife once donated $20 million to Spelman College, a black institution of higher learning in Atlanta.

Cosby. A comedian with advanced degrees in education, Cosby was the first African-American to be a featured player in a network series. He used that fame to star in Saturday-morning television for kids, nightclub routines, and, in 1984, in NBC-TV's "The Bill Cosby Show."

Cosby portrayed a physician living in New York City with a smart, handsome, witty, and loving family. They knew and read good books, they snacked on healthy foods, they appreciated all kinds of music; the children were, of course, headed for college, and there were never hints of the deteriorating lives of many black people living in the country at the time. Dad Bill Cosby was a lovable guy everyone outsmarted, and Mom was the lawyer backbone of the family. The thirty-minute program on Thursday evenings zoomed to the top spot in the ratings and remained there for many years.

The eighties saw numerous firsts. Ted Koppel began "Nightline," an intelligent news show that came on ABC affiliates after the nightly local news. Opposite him, on NBC, was Johnny Carson, followed, in 1982, by the goofy, irreverent David Letterman. "Dynasty," a prime-time soap opera on CBS, started in 1981 and was important because it featured more mature actors and actresses than usual in leading roles. The realistic police show, "Hill Street Blues," began rather slowly on NBC that same year, then picked up fans. MTV introduced nonstop rock videos via cable in 1983, and Showtime delivered movies around the clock to cable subscribers.

The year 1984 marked the debut of "Miami Vice." Gone were earth tones — in their place were watery, bright shades of pink and aqua. The tropical tints were mixed with outrageous violence in stories about a city that needed no extra bad publicity. "The Golden Girls" came along in 1985, starring matronly women in a comedy with wide audience appeal. "L.A. Law" debuted in 1986, "Thirtysomething" showed up in 1987, and "Roseanne" thundered onto the screen in 1988. That same year, Ted Turner offered cable viewers TNT, a vintage movie channel. And, in 1989, these talk show hosts flooded the air: Oprah Winfrey, Phil Donahue, Geraldo Rivera, Sally Jesse Raphael, Pat Sajak, Morton Downey, Jr., Arsenio Hall, Sonya Friedman, and Larry King.

There was something familiar about all this talk — similar formats had helped make AM radio viable. AM radio seemed to attract conservative, older, more religious and less educated listeners, and a talkative young man by the name of Rush Limbaugh was ready to entertain them. He, Pat Buchanan, and G. Gordon Liddy all were syndicated to hundreds of stations, where they attracted sizeable audiences by attacking women, liberals, and environmentalists. Ironically, surveys showed that only small percentages of their audiences ever bothered to vote.

The three main television networks, in contrast, gradually began to lose their grip on mass audiences. "Channel surfers," individuals who sample dozens of programs on network stations and on cable without stopping for any length of time, diluted the value of advertising. Perhaps because of this, some firms tried shorter commercials, lasting as little as fifteen seconds, while others created advertising that told a continu-

Connie Chung.

Broadcast journalist Connie Chung was born and reared in Washington, D.C. She was sheltered from much of the news by being the youngest member of a large and close-knit Chinese-American family. The family came to America in 1944, and Connie was the only daughter born in the United States.

She grew up in a Maryland suburb, where classmates remember her as quiet but willing to try out for high school plays and variety shows. After doing publicity for a political campaign one summer during college, she switched her major at the University of Maryland from biology to journalism. Following graduation in 1969, she worked as a news department secretary at a local TV station, advancing to the positions of newswriter, assignment editor, and on-air reporter.

Chung applied for a job in 1971 with the CBS Washington bureau. That year, CBS hired a Chinese-American woman (Chung), an African-American woman (Michelle Clark), a Jewish woman (Sylvia Chase), and a white woman (Leslie Stahl)! "They took care of years of discrimination," Chung once told a reporter with a wry smile.

Chung covered antiwar protests, congressional hearings, the McGovern presidential campaign, and the Watergate political scandal. She also accompanied Richard Nixon on foreign trips, and she learned how to throw tough questions at the mighty as well as the meek.

In 1976, she accepted the position of local news anchor in Los Angeles on the CBS affiliate. Her salary climbed from about $27,000 to approximately $600,000 in the next seven years. She won several local awards, but she wanted to cover the 1984 presidential campaign and national politics, so NBC signed her up and she returned to the East Coast, this time as a "Nightly News" reporter and Saturday anchor.

Chung had a succession of jobs at NBC, from an early-morning anchor on "NBC News at Sunrise" to cohost, with Roger Mudd, on a news-feature show called "American Almanac." She served as a substitute on the "Today" show for Jane Pauley, and she pinch-hit for Tom Brokaw, who anchored "NBC Nightly News." From 1987 to 1989, she cowrote and hosted several prime-time documentaries. She even went to China, where she had a tearful meeting with relatives she had never seen before.

She rejoined CBS in 1989, reportedly for $1.5 million per year. Chung denies that she is a workaholic, but she admits to getting by on about six hours of sleep each night.

ing story. Someone invented thirty-minute "infomercials," scripted programs that looked like game or talk shows but which in fact sold products or services.

A fourth network, Fox, was introduced in 1987. It began with just seven stations, but eventually became available, via cable and independent broadcasters, in more than 90 percent of U.S. homes. "The Simpsons," Fox's cynical cartoon series, rose to challenge Bill Cosby on Thursday evenings, and "In

Paul "Pee-Wee Herman" Reubens.

The officer at the desk in the Florida police station looked at the small, unkempt man with long, stringy hair who had just been brought in. He looked again. "Hey, guys, we caught Pee-Wee Herman!" So they had.

Paul Reubens, the comedian who played Pee-Wee Herman, was a Florida native who in the early eighties began to portray an innocent and childlike young man. Reubens' first movie, *Pee-Wee's Big Adventure*, was a 1985 hit. After that came a Saturday morning television series viewed by children and adults and a second hit movie, *Big Top Pee-Wee*, in 1988.

Reubens had hit on a good thing. Although he was thirty-five years old in 1988, he convincingly looked and acted like a wholesome, short-haired, rosy-cheeked, nerdy boy who had not yet reached puberty. Pee-Wee was an innocent person who succeeded in the world despite efforts by mean people and seductive women to steer him off course. He was called hip, corny, and avant-garde.

The arrest in Florida, for exposing himself in public in the vicinity of an adult-video store, apparently ended his career. Pee-Wee and Reubens himself are important for several reasons: The character was entertaining to children and adults, providing a shared experience, even if the experience came straight from the screen. Plus, Reubens's downfall was a real contrast to the character he played, leading some to wonder if wearing funny clothes and dressing up animals pushed him toward antisocial behavior.

Paul Reubens (second from left) with fellow comics (from left to right) Chris Rock, Howie Mandel, and Joan Rivers.

The World of Books

Books were one of the competitors for people's leisure time, and the gap between bestselling books and great books continued to widen. Only two writers connected to the U.S. won Nobel Prizes for literature during the decade, and neither Czeslaw Milosz in 1980 nor Joseph Brodsky in 1987 could claim that they were widely read or that America was their native land. Nevertheless, an American by the name of Raymond Carver proved that a writer could be both an artist and enjoy popularity. Carver did it with as few words as possible.

Raymond Carver was a minimalist. In other words, he used short, to-the-point sentences and spare descriptions to tell of his fictional characters. And what characters! The heroes and heroines in Carver's short stories are everyone's not-so-lucky rel-

Living Color" served up noisy African-American humor on Sunday nights. Preteens and teenagers watched and approved of everything from "Beverly Hills 90210," about well-to-do high school students, to new and offbeat cartoon shows.

atives or neighbors. They are a man wasting time after being sentenced but before heading off for prison, a woman forced to sell a red convertible due to bankruptcy, a couple snooping in a vacationing neighbor's house, and so on. Raymond Carver's characters were the faceless men and women who inhabited the middle and lower-middle classes all over the country.

Carver, who died of cancer in 1988 at the age of fifty, gained fame with several story collections, including *Where I'm Calling From* (1988), *What We Talk About When We Talk About Love* (1981), and *Will You Please Be Quiet, Please* (1976). He was called the greatest short-story writer by British and American critics during his brief life, and he seemed the perfect antidote to fiction that was more interested in words than in real life.

Toni Morrison.

Lorain, Ohio, isn't the tidiest place on earth. But the gritty town west of Cleveland has produced lots of Ford cars, Great Lakes ships, college athletes, and at least one stunning novelist, Toni Morrison. Born Chloe Anthony Morrison on a winter day in 1931, Morrison showed very early that she had a superior intelligence. She graduated from Howard University in 1953, then earned an advanced degree at Cornell University. She was hired to teach English and humanities at Texas Southern University briefly before Howard lured her back to Washington, D.C., where she taught for seven years.

But Random House, the huge New York City publisher, learned of her writing talent and hired her in 1965 as an editor and then as a senior editor. She was there twenty years, editing the work of others as she perfected her own fiction. Among numerous accomplishments, she helped showcase the talents of fellow African-American authors. Her most popular 1980s book, *Beloved*, won not only the Pulitzer Prize but the Robert F. Kennedy and Melcher book awards. Besides six novels, she has written a book of literary criticism.

Divorced and the mother of two sons, Morrison has been called the best living black writer by *Newsweek*, which featured her in a cover story. After *Song of Solomon* won the National Book Critics Circle Award in 1970, Morrison served as the Albert Schweitzer Professor of the Humanities at the State University of New York at Albany. Her first drama, *Dreaming Emmett*, about a black fourteen-year-old killed in Mississippi in the 1950s, was produced at the Market Theater in Albany in 1986.

Readers dig into Morrison's books because her work is immensely interesting. That is also why, beginning in 1989, she has taught a course at Princeton University that is an intriguing mix of creative writing, African studies, and women's studies. She is, said the *New York Times*, a "Big Name on Campus."

Luckily, there were several other important writers in the 1980s, though few are as hard to forget as Carver.

One is Larry McMurtry, the Texan who wrote many different kinds of novels very well, from *Lone-*

Alice Walker was a social worker, teacher, and lecturer before she won the Pulitzer Prize in 1982 for her novel The Color Purple, *the story of two sisters in the Deep South between the wars. An acclaimed poet, short story writer, biographer, and essayist, Walker melds together politics, women's issues, the African-American experience, and a strong sense of connection to both the past and the future in her writing.*

some Dove to *Hud*. Another was Robert Stone, who won a National Book Award in the 1970s with a haunting, Vietnam-influenced book called *Dog Soldiers* and has since written half a dozen books almost as good. No one worked harder or had more consistent results than Don DeLillo, author of *White Noise* and other solid fiction, much of it satire. Two African-American women, Alice Walker and Toni Morrison, wrote fiction that both focused on and soared above the country's ongoing racial problems to deliver universal truths. Other prominent writers in the eight-

ies included William Kennedy (*Iron-weed*), Joyce Carol Oates (*A Bloodsmoor Romance*, and *Mysteries of Winterthorn*), Anne Tyler (*Breathing Lessons*) and John Updike (*Rabbit is Rich*). Updike topped literary lists for more than three decades, employing themes of death, sex, and spirituality.

Meanwhile, there were bestsellers aplenty, trashy and otherwise. Quality nonfiction was represented by *A Brief History of Time*, a book that explained how the heavens got there by British scientist Stephen Hawking. Equally fascinating, and with an engaging title, was *The Man Who Mistook His Wife for a Hat*. This account of brain-injured patients was written by psychiatrist Oliver Sacks. Business books were winners, too, with *In Search of Excellence*, by Thomas J. Peters and Robert H. Waterman, Jr., a typical example. Another success of the decade was *The Far Side*, a cartoon of animals and grotesque humans doing silly things, drawn by Gary Larson, which appeared in many newspapers. As for junk reading, a series of *Truly Tasteless Jokes* by someone calling herself Blanche Knott competed for readers early in the decade. Later on, a paperback favorite would be made up of late-night television entertainer David Letterman's *Top 10 Lists*.

Art and Architecture

In the art world, the magic word was money. Auctions held at New York City's two major art-auction houses in 1983 totaled an astonishing $67 million. Artists of the past weren't the only ones to be noticed. The works of contemporary painters such as Jasper Johns were in great demand. A newspaper magnate in

1988 paid $17.7 million for a Johns painting, *False Start*. In fairness to the art world, it should be pointed out that prices for all sorts of collectibles skyrocketed during the decade. Cars, dolls, teddy bears, buttons, baseball cards, military memorabilia, rare books — these and other items were ferreted out and purchased by enthusiastic fans. But little could compare to prices paid for fine art, which proved there was a real elite in this country and that it was doing very, very well.

Art made news in 1986, when it was discovered that famed painter Andrew Wyeth had painted 246 portraits of one of his Pennsylvania neighbors. The blonde, fifty-year-old woman had posed, usually nude, for fifteen years so that an anonymous collector who admired both Wyeth and the model could be satisfied.

Art's most impressive achievements were in postmodern architecture. There was significant big-building construction of offices, apartments, and institutions. Designers of these dramatic, downtown facilities included Michael Graves, Philip Johnson, and Stanley Tigerman. Their buildings were a blend of geometric designs and traditional decorations. An excellent example begun in the late 1980s is the Harold Washington Memorial Library in Chicago.

Graves, a teacher at Princeton University, designed a teakettle-shaped addition to New York City's Whitney Museum of American Art. He drew on classic architecture from all around the Mediterranean Sea, employing columns, pyramids, keystones, and vaults to create buildings that appeared classical and postmodern at the same time. He also was conscious of color, often leaving his creations white or painting the lower portions terra cotta and the upper portions sky blue. Graves submitted two radical designs for the $37.5 million Whitney Museum addition before a toned-down version, one that would not overshadow the museum itself, was accepted.

Television Rules Sports

In sports, cable television delivered every conceivable kind of contest in a twenty-four-hours-a-day, seven-days-a-week effort to offer almost anything at all to watch. ESPN became the most popular cable channel, with nearly sixty million subscribers by the decade's end. Consequently, sports such as water polo or volleyball, and pseudosports such as professional wrestling exhibitions and monster-truck demonstrations gained large audiences. Boxing, automobile and motorcycle racing, horse racing, karate, kickboxing, and events even more obscure were broadcast for paying viewers. Also the beneficiaries of added exposure were college basketball and football teams.

The three networks, ABC, CBS, and NBC, continued to pay incredible sums to broadcast top contests in professional baseball, basketball, and football. Players' representatives noted the huge sums being paid to major league sports and successfully negotiated wonderful long-term contracts on behalf of their clients. One of the most amazing things about the 1980s is that fans grumbled but never staged any sort of boycott over the obscene amounts of money paid to many so-so athletes. Not even labor-management fights involving baseball in 1981 and football in 1982 resulted

Martina Navratilova.

Martina Navratilova has won more professional tennis singles championships than any other woman. That is just one mark in a career that began half a world away and reached its peak in the United States in the 1980s.

Born in Czechoslovakia in 1956, Navratilova entered the U.S. in 1975, the same year she switched from amateur to professional tennis playing, and became a naturalized citizen in 1981. By then, she was in a class by herself. "The first time I saw Martina," remembers fellow pro Jimmy Connors, "her look was different, her game was different, her body was different. I know what she's had to do to get from there to where she is today, all the hard work, all the conditioning. Along the way, she changed women's tennis."

Navratilova worked very hard and it paid off. She won the world's most prestigious singles title, Wimbledon, nine times — six of the nine during the 1980s. She has won the Virginia Slims of Chicago tournament a dozen times. And she has won everywhere else, beating whichever women were best at the time, including Chris Evert.

An admitted lesbian, Martina was among the first stars in any sport to let her sexual preference be known. It was heavily suspected, anyway, since at least one of her live-in companions filed suit in 1989 for half of all the assets the tennis star had accumulated during the six years in which the two had lived together.

Named the Associated Press Female Athlete of the Year in 1983, the Czech native wears a lot of gold and enjoys driving her Porsche. She has won millions of dollars and tons of metal in the form of trophies. Navratilova's game remained powerful and exciting all decade long because of her commitment to staying in top condition.

in a loss of interest by their fans.

If football and baseball kept up their popularity, professional basketball took a quantum leap forward due to such exciting players as Larry Byrd, Magic Johnson, and, above all, Michael Jordan. Beginning in 1985, Jordan soared above the rims in huge arenas all across the country to star as a member of the Chicago Bulls. Besides winning the National Basketball Association's scoring title from 1986 through 1992, Jordan was named most valuable player three times and led his team to two championships. He all but overshadowed the first of the high-flying basketball dunkers, the great Julius Erving. Erving retired in 1987.

Part of Jordan's popularity could be attributed to the immediacy of television. Brilliant camera work made basketball almost bounce into American living rooms as huge, gifted men, almost all of whom were African-American, slammed dunk shots and sank lofty three-point baskets. Football and baseball also televised well, and all three sports had the sense to massage their rules for the best possible presentation to a TV audience. Championship games in all three sports are shown during prime-time hours, and football's annual Super Bowl has consistently drawn among the largest audiences ever to watch any televised show or event.

Colleges became aware of the immense amounts of money available from football games and went to court about it. The Supreme Court ruled seven-to-two in 1984 that the

Michael Jordan was a member of the U. S. basketball team that won the Olympic title in 1984. He went on to become the most exciting player in the National Basketball Association's (NBA) history.

Joe Montana.

Like more football players than anyone cares to name, Joseph C. Montana, Jr., was born into a blue-collar, Pennsylvania family of Italian heritage. He grew up in the small town of New Eagle, pitching a football to anyone who would catch it. Montana went on to quarterback for his high school team and then to star for the University of Notre Dame in South Bend, Indiana.

Montana was drafted into the professional National Football League in 1978 by the San Francisco 49ers. One of the original pro football squads, the 49ers were colorful and sometimes exciting but did not often win as many games as they lost. The young man with the sure arm took over the role of starting quarterback at the same time the innovative Bill Walsh was named head coach.

Within three years, Montana and his mates were facing the Dallas Cowboys in the National Football Conference game that would propel one of them into the Super Bowl. With little time remaining, Montana directed a tremendous drive and then lofted a pass to wide receiver Dwight Clark in the end zone. It was a victory from which the Cowboys would not recover during the 1980s.

Montana and the 49ers went on to win the Super Bowl in 1982 — and in 1985, 1988, and 1990. The quarterback, often playing with pain from injuries inflicted by an opposing defensive unit, was named the Super Bowl's Most Valuable Player in 1982, 1985, and 1990. In 1989, he was named MVP for the entire league.

The game took its toll on Montana. Nevertheless, he was one of the highest-paid and best-performing players ever to put on a football jersey. His ability to conceal where he intended to throw the football until the last possible moment helped his team consistently score more points than its foe, pack stadiums at home or away, and thrill millions of Americans in front of the TV.

National Collegiate Athletic Association had violated federal antitrust laws by preventing individual schools from negotiating the rights to their telecasts. Some schools, such as Notre Dame and Oklahoma, had wider followings than others. Yet the NCAA had funneled similar amounts of money to those universities as was handed to schools with lesser talent. The only question following the Supreme Court ruling was this: To what ends would a college go to have a winning team? "There's a thin line between football players and hoodlums," said one college professor.

The 1980s saw the creation of professional football's very first

Florence Griffith Joyner. (1959-1998)

"FloJo," as she has come to be called, won three gold medals and a silver medal as a sprinter in the 1988 Olympics. She did it with speed and a great deal of style.

Griffith was born in a small town in California's Mojave Desert. The seventh of eleven children, she and her brothers and sisters moved when she was still young to the tough Watts section of inner-city Los Angeles. A mother who was a strict disciplinarian and an early urge to run track kept Griffith out of trouble, and she began winning important track meets while still in junior high school. Simultaneously, she showed that she was a real individual — she kept a pet boa constrictor snake, and she began to design and make her own clothing and accessories.

Griffith attended California State University for a year, then dropped out due to lack of money. Her track coach at California State, Bob Kersee, helped her find financial aid, and she enrolled at the University of California at Los Angeles (UCLA) when Kersee went there as a track coach. She just missed qualifying for the 1980 Olympics, then won the National Collegiate Athletic Association (NCAA) two-hundred-meter dash in 1982. In 1984, she finished second to teammate Valerie Briscoe in the Olympics held in Los Angeles, earning a silver medal. Wherever she ran, she showed up in eye-catching clothes and a rainbow of paint on her nails.

Working days as a banker and nights as a beautician, Griffith got out of shape. But in 1987, she asked Kersee to help her train for the 1988 Olympic trials. He put her on a diet, forced her to work out before and after her jobs, and introduced her to weight training. Meanwhile, the flamboyant runner met and married Al Joyner, winner of the triple-jump gold medal in the 1984 Olympics and the brother of track star Jackie Joyner-Kersee.

At the Olympic trials in July 1988, Joyner showed up in a lime green, one-legged racing suit! More important, she clicked off four separate one hundred-meter runs at incredible speeds. The following day, in a black body suit with yellow stripes, and then in a one-legged blue leotard and white bikini, she won two more one hundred-meter runs. Later, in a fishnet suit, she took the semifinals and the finals in the two hundred-meter sprint.

Florence Griffith Joyner became a media sensation, appearing on the covers of dozens of magazines. Suddenly, she was commanding appearance money at track meets to the tune of $25,000! She continued to rewrite the record books at the Olympics in Seoul, winning gold medals in one hundred-meter and two hundred-meter runs, and in the four hundred-meter relay. At the end of 1988, she won the Sullivan Award as America's top amateur athlete.

Joyner announced her retirement in 1989 in order to devote time to writing and acting. She was a spokesperson for many different companies, and appeared in many commercials. The triple gold medalist, who captivated the world with her speed and style, died in her sleep on September 21, 1998, of a heart seizure. She was thirty-eight years old.

million-dollar player. Herschel Walker, a running back with the University of Georgia, skipped his senior year of college to sign a three-year pact in 1983 for an estimated $5 million with the New Jersey Generals of the United States Football League. Though the league lasted only three seasons, Walker was paid the full amount and then went on to a career in the established National Football League.

Consumer Pitches

One of the consequences of such spectaculars is that fans knew and followed professional athletes as never before. Should a fan happen to miss a big game, chances are the starring quarterback or forward or pitcher would be seen anyhow in fifteen- or thirty-second commercials. Other sports, such as golf and tennis, had a following, but none compared to baseball, basketball, or football. Sports such as hockey or soccer, which were harder to follow on television, failed to capture the U.S. imagination, even though hockey stars such as Wayne Gretzky and Mario Lemieux were the equal of athletes in any other contest.

Sporting events, and conjecture over who would win them, resulted in a rise in sports gambling throughout the period. Lotteries, which were held in thirty-two of the fifty states by 1990, also competed for consumer dollars. Lotteries were run by states at the insistence of voters who saw nothing wrong with gambling and felt the profits could pay for schools or perhaps slow the rise in property taxes. Though the lotteries had deposited $8.5 billion into various state treasuries by 1990, taxes continued their climb. The major difference

for consumers was that they sometimes took their supermarket or convenience-store change in lottery tickets. Several lottery jackpots, in places such as Florida and Illinois, paid each winner as much as $50 million — which was subject to tax!

More traditional gambling venues also did well. Las Vegas began to change its image from a glitzy gulch run by gangsters to a family-oriented vacation spot. New Jersey's nine casinos in Atlantic City reported winnings totaling $1.77 billion in 1983, compared to the approximately $2 billion won in the ninety casinos in and around Las Vegas. Such figures did not go unnoticed — places such as Galveston, Texas, and riverboat towns along the Mississippi in Iowa began offering casino-style gambling, while Indian reservations lured gamblers with bingo and casino games.

So Much for Culture

A prominent American writer, Philip Roth, estimated during the 1980s that there were only 120,000 readers of serious literature in the entire United States. Looking at the way Americans amused themselves during the decade, that figure might have been optimistic! For every visitor to an art gallery, there were thousands of patrons at a videocassette rental store. For every ticket sold for a symphony, there was an avalanche of tickets sold for lotteries. And for every collection of poems toted home, there were hundreds of drippy, predictable romance novels. Though they complained constantly that taxes took all their disposable income, Americans kept finding new ways to dispose of it all by themselves.

CHAPTER 7
Iran-contra and Other Scandals

But for a helicopter crash, the whole Iran-contra scandal might never have occurred. That accident in 1981, of unknown cause, took the life of General Omar Torrijos, the leader of Panama at the time. There followed in the tiny, Central American country a struggle that ended with General Manuel Noriega becoming the nation's dictator. Noriega's ethics were as scarred as his ravaged face: He was willing to sell anything and everything to the highest bidder.

In fairness to U.S. foreign policy, it should be pointed out that America initially tried legally to oust the Panamanian dictator by simply pressuring him. After that failed, the U.S. secretly paid off Noriega. The Central Intelligence Agency (CIA) arranged to sell arms to the strongman, supposedly to protect Panama, but in truth as a way to funnel guns to Nicaragua's antigovernment contras. The contras were Nicaraguans who disliked the fact that a Communist government had taken over their native land. They took to the hills and pleaded for aid from wealthy, conservative Americans within and outside the government. Noriega was all too willing to let his country serve as pipeline for U.S. money and guns to the contras.

Unfortunately, the Panamanian leader had made a similar arrangement with the Colombian drug cartel, powerful and ruthless traffickers in marijuana and cocaine. Drug lords living in and around the Colombian city of Medellin tortured and killed their enemies, many of whom were government officials they could not bribe. More than half of all cocaine entering the United States in the 1980s came from the cartel, whose vicious members did not care that their illegal substances were destroying American lives.

During Ronald Reagan's third and fourth years as president, individuals in the White House and several employees of the CIA, along with the Israelis, conspired to send arms made in Yugoslavia to Panama, for eventual shipment to Nicaragua. It was essential that the weapons came from a Communist country because the contras then could claim they had captured the arms from Nicaragua's army. Contra forces also were trained on Panamanian soil, a deal arranged by Marine Lieutenant Colonel Oliver L. North, a member of Reagan's National Security Council.

The sordid mess was known as early as 1983, but it did not really begin to unravel until the fall of 1986. A Panamanian civil defense plane carrying arms to the contras crashed in Nicaragua and was followed by the shooting down of an American cargo plane, also used to fly arms to rebels supported by the United States. One of the four crew members of the American plane, Eugene Hasenfus, survived. He

POLITICS

For further information see primary source entries on pages

11: 1482-83; **12:** 1603-04, 1620-24, 1632-35, 1682-85, 1688-89, 1692-94, 1700-01, 1706-09, 1727-30

General Manuel Noriega at a rally of his supporters in Panama City, celebrating his defeat of an attempt to oust him from power in October 1989. Soon afterwards, the U.S. invaded Panama to arrest him for his part in the smuggling of drugs from South America to the U.S. Earlier in the decade, the Reagan administration had been happy to have his cooperation and help in getting arms to the contra rebels in Nicaragua.

walked away from the crash of the cargo plane because he had been the only person to pack a parachute. Unfortunately, he walked into Nicaraguan soldiers, who took him captive, grilled him about his work, and put him on display. Hasenfus told the Nicaragua government that he had been recruited by friends in Vietnam who had remained U.S. government employees after Hasenfus left Asia to return to civilian life.

Naming Names

Hasenfus provided the Nicaraguan government with names, places, and facts. One of the names he offered was that of Max Gomez, an alias for a Cuban-American who had been deeply involved in the ill-fated Bay of Pigs invasion of Cuba. Gomez, whose real name was Rodriguez, had met with Vice President George Bush several times prior to the capture of Hasenfus. Though Bush would always deny knowledge of the entire deal, one notation in his appointment book indicated the purpose of a meeting with Gomez/Rodriguez was to discuss "resupply of the contras." No wonder William Casey, director of the CIA at the time, told White House advisors to shred documents.

George Shultz, who was secreatery of state from 1982 to 1989, denied American involvement in moving arms into Nicaragua because he was one of the few Reagan insiders unaware of the arms deal. Because some Reagan advisors knew that Shultz would not approve of the deal, they authorized support of the contras without telling him. People such as Secretary of Defense Caspar Weinberger and Vice President Bush

knew and participated in the plot, but Shultz did not. He believed the air crews were "hired by private people."

Oliver North tried to control the damage to White House insiders by telling FBI investigators that the operation was a secret mission ordered by the president. He told the U.S. Customs Service, which was on the trail of CIA gunrunners in Florida, that those involved had done nothing illegal. Others, including advisors John Poindexter and Robert McFarlane, called the attorney general, Ed Meese, to get him to distract various law enforcement personnel. They told Meese and FBI Director William Webster that there was an "Iran initiative" involved and that investigations could do it major harm. Webster delayed the FBI probe for several days.

A former economics professor, member of the Nixon administration, and corporate executive, George P. Shultz was secretary of state from 1982 to 1989. A moderate politician and a supporter of arms control, he helped improve U. S. relations with the Soviet Union. Schultz was one of the few Reagan insiders unaware of the arms deal with the contras.

Oliver North.

The U.S. Marine lieutenant colonel was out of uniform. Oliver North was discovered by police roaming a Virginia suburb without any clothes but carrying a pistol one night in 1974. During psychiatric treatment, he blamed the incident on delayed stress from Vietnam combat. However, such behavior calls into question whether North was in fact a "loose cannon" rolling around the deck of the ship of state during the Reagan years.

North was born in 1943, the son of a World War II veteran. He grew up in rural New York, attended the U.S. Naval Academy, and received a commission as a marine officer. He learned to love guerilla-type operations in Vietnam, where opinion on him was sharply divided. Some felt he was a wonderful leader, while others noted that he shamelessly kissed up to superiors, exaggerated his own importance, and was incapable of questioning even the stupidest order. He returned to the U.S. with numerous medals, full of ambition.

Joining President Reagan's National Security Council, North shuffled papers until some time in 1983, when he and several members and friends of the CIA began to direct the running of guns into Nicaragua for that country's anticommunist rebels. When such illegal acts, which were hidden from Congress, began to come apart, the Reagan administration attempted to pin everything on North — and on the CIA's director, William Casey, who died of cancer in 1987.

North gained national attention by appearing before congressional investigators to proclaim that he was simply following orders. He reported briefing both President Reagan and Vice President Bush regularly about the complex covert operation, which involved moving weapons and cash from continent to continent and from country to country.

Portrayed by his attorney as Ronald Reagan's sacrificial lamb, North nevertheless was convicted in a Washington, D.C., court of falsifying and destroying documents, accepting hush money, and obstructing Congress. He was sentenced to twelve hundred hours of community service in a drug-prevention program but did not serve one day in jail. The marine's sentence was overturned in 1990 by a three-judge panel voting two to one to acquit. Both judges voting in North's favor were Reagan appointees.

Ever the self-promoter, North spent the late 1980s acquiring wealth by giving speeches before conservative organizations. He was especially pleased when the three judges threw out his convictions because, now free of the charges, he could run for political office. He plans to run for the U.S. Senate.

As if the schemers didn't have enough problems, CIA Director Casey was being blackmailed. He had helped arrange the sale of arms to Iranians in exchange for the release of hostages, and two Canadian arms dealers who had not been paid threatened to talk. They demanded $10 million. This deal, in which Iran paid the United States for weapons, was cut apparently so Iran could fight its next-door neighbor and mortal enemy, Iraq. TOW missiles, Hawk missiles, and other weapons were sold to the Iranians, and in return, the Iranians were able to persuade Muslim terrorists to release American hostages.

This deal had several strange twists. President Reagan insisted repeatedly throughout his presidency that the United States would not negotiate with terrorists. He even attempted in 1983 to persuade allies to stop sending arms to Iran because it was a country that supported terrorism. But in reality, arms were secretly sold to the Iranians by the U.S., which so overcharged for the weapons that the sizeable profits went to buy arms for the contras! Congress, receiving hints all along of illegal and unconstitutional deals, needed a scorecard to keep up with such free enterprise gone wrong.

A Legacy of Intervention

The United States had been interested in Nicaragua in varying degrees for most of the century, with U.S. Marines landing more than once to restore order. Beginning in the 1960s, order hinged on an American-appointed dictator, General Anastasio Somoza. The people of Nicaragua paid little attention to Somoza's Communist-leaning opposition until a violent earthquake shook the country in 1972. Somoza and his cronies accepted millions in emergency relief — and kept it for themselves. More and more middle-class people joined workers in backing the guerrilla group, known as the Sandinista National Liberation Front. They drove Somoza out, seeing to it that he was executed in Paraguay in 1980.

The guerrillas were allied with Cuba and were opposed by former Somoza soldiers, who became known as the contras, along with the civilians mentioned earlier. The United States started arming the contras as early as 1981, encouraging a civil war that as often as not resulted in the deaths of more civilians than combatants. Desperately poor, Nicaragua tried to rebuild as the CIA helped combat the new government under President Daniel Ortega. The CIA did everything from mining Nicaraguan harbors to creating a military training manual, despite a decision by Congress not to actively interfere in the small country's problems or provide support for the contras.

The Violence Spreads

The contest between Nicaragua and the U.S. spilled over into neighboring El Salvador shortly before the 1984 presidential election. The Soviet Union had shipped arms to Cuba, the Cubans shipped the arms to Nicaragua, and the Nicaraguans provided the fellow revolutionaries next door with the weapons. Violence spread in Central America, with news reporters, priests, nuns, and other Americans among its victims. The violence was, of course, inflicted much more seriously and more often on the local people of the region.

The war in El Salvador would continue throughout the decade, resulting in fifty thousand deaths — in a tiny country of only five million residents. Communist sympathizers controlled about one-quarter of the country, and were opposed most strongly by right-wing death squads organized to eliminate leftist sympathizers in parts of the country still under government control. The death squads combined police, civilian, and military forces. Fortunately, a moderate member of the Christian

"We did not — repeat, did not — trade weapons or anything else for hostages — nor will we."

Ronald Reagan, 1986

"A few months ago, I told the American people I did not trade arms for hostages. My heart and best intentions still tell me this is true, but the facts and the evidence tell me it is not."

Ronald Reagan, 1987

Democrat party by the name of Jose Napoleon Duarte was elected with 54 percent of the vote in 1984, leading to the end of El Salvador's civil war eight years later.

Fallout from America's Covert Actions

A prosecutor by the name of Lawrence Walsh was chosen in 1986 to sort out America's role in the Iran-contra affair, and it took him seven years to do so and make the results public. Walsh and his cadre of lawyers decided that Ronald Reagan set the stage for the illegal activities and that George Bush failed to tell the truth about his knowledge and involvement. Attorneys for Reagan and Bush of course denied the findings.

Specifically, the report said President Reagan created an atmosphere in which aides felt free to act outside the law. It further stated that Reagan's comments to people such as Oliver North were an "invitation to break the law." Since North apparently had no sense of right or wrong when it came to the wishes of his superiors, this is a believable conclusion. And since George Bush was head of the CIA before becoming vice president, it's hard to see how he could possibly have been left out of this ongoing conspiracy.

Several unanswered questions might have come to light in the trial of Caspar Weinberger, the secretary of defense. But Bush pardoned Weinberger and five other Iran-contra figures just before leaving office in 1992. Questions that might have been

Guerillas fire at the Salvadoran army in San Miguel in November 1989. A ferocious civil war took place in El Salvador from 1984 to 1992, as President José Napoleon Duarte tried to implement social and economic reforms, while opposed by both right-wing and left-wing guerillas.

Robert McFarlane, a former national security advisor, testifies before the House Foreign Affairs Committee, in December 1986, that President Reagan authorized an indirect shipment of arms to Iran in August 1985. Ironically, in 1983, Reagan had tried to stop other countries from sending arms to Iran because, he said, the Iranians supported terrorism.

answered included whether men around the president engaged in a cover-up to shield Reagan from possible impeachment. Among those blamed in Walsh's report were former Attorney General Ed Meese, and Robert M. Gates, head of the CIA at the time, who was accused of knowing North had contact with the contras. But Gates avoided a trial because of a lack of evidence.

Students of the law and of politics read the final Iran-contra report with interest. But, by the time it was published, it was old news. Today's and tomorrow's news had ways of making yesterday's events much less interesting — even when the integrity of presidents Ronald Reagan and George Bush was called into question. There was one other matter — no one looked forward to reliving the events leading up to impeachment. People in and out of government remembered the summer of 1974, Watergate, and Richard Nixon and decided not to press on.

Scandals Everywhere

There were other scandals during the Reagan years. The Wedtech scandal involved influence peddling, bribes, government contracts, kickbacks, fraud, conspiracy, and national defense. It also involved Attorney General Ed Meese, White House staff member Lyn Nofziger, and other people of various ranks in the Reagan administration.

Wedtech was a machine shop on the brink of bankruptcy in South Bronx, New York. After failing to win defense contracts by competing honestly, Wedtech called on people in high places to exert their influence, thereby getting Wedtech contracts for which no one else bid. Wedtech gained access to the innermost dealings of Washington by hiring friends of Ed Meese. More than that, Meese, Nofziger, and others pressured the army to reconsider Wedtech for contracts already turned down for being too costly.

Wedtech received defense contracts, loans, and grants. It was suddenly worth a lot of money, and it issued stock to those who had assisted the company. The bubble burst when Wedtech was accused of insider trading by the Securities and Exchange Commission and the Small Business Administration dropped the firm from its minority-business program. Nofziger was fined and jailed, but Meese proved to be "unindictable," although he left office fairly quickly.

Wedtech was the tip of a rotten iceberg. Year after year, dozens of questionable deals were put together by and for the Department of Defense as the portion of the federal budget aimed at protecting the country continued to grow. Federal investigations into Pentagon dealings numbered in the dozens. Between 1983 and 1985, there were twelve separate official probes against one major defense contractor alone. Because members of

Congress were fighting for their share of defense contracts for industries back home, oversight by Congress was poor.

But perhaps the most heartless scandal of all involved the Department of Housing and Urban Development (HUD). There, friends of the influential became rich by depriving the poor — the very people HUD's housing money was designed to help. They did so in several ways, though one common method was to charge huge consulting fees to contractors and other clients who wanted to receive HUD money with which to build. James Watt, the former secretary of the interior, admitted to a congressional committee that he received a huge sum by making phone calls on behalf of his friends to people high up in the Reagan administration.

Part of the problem was Samuel Pierce, head of HUD and the highest-ranking African-American in the administration. The former Wall Street

In June 1989, Deborah Gore Dean, a top aide to former Housing and Urban Development Secretary Samuel Pierce, refuses to answer questions from a House panel probing the housing scandal. Pierce himself also refused to testify, having tried several times to avoid the investigators.

James Watt.

Until James Watt was named secretary of the interior, the cabinet-level post had always been held by someone who was at least on friendly terms with environmental groups. Not so James Watt — he had served development interests as an attorney, and he distrusted and disliked people who wanted to preserve unspoiled federal land.

A westerner himself, Watt was also a Christian always ready to share his views. On one occasion, he said, "We have abandoned the political role to the religious left. . . . We have seen government used by the enemies of liberty and freedom here in America, God's chosen place."

As secretary of the interior, James Watt wanted to develop previously untouched federal acreage. He openly defied a U.S. House of Representatives' ban on federal coal leasing by putting up for auction 540 million tons of such coal in Montana and North Dakota in 1983. The Senate quickly voted to stop the selling of coal leases for six months, in part because Watt had engineered a 1982 coal-lease sale in Montana and Wyoming that had sold for millions below fair market value.

Watt, who sincerely believed that the land could be used in any way since the end of the world was near, also had other problems. He made an insensitive remark in September 1983 about a group of people serving on an independent commission studying coal-lease policies. Watt said that the commission had "three Democrats, two Republicans, every kind of mix you can have. I have a black, a woman, two Jews, and a cripple."

The remark infuriated people. Watt's views had found only lukewarm support on Capitol Hill all along among Republicans, so when Democrats wanted to throw him out, they were not alone. Watt apologized for what he called a clumsy attempt at humor, but members of the GOP distanced themselves from him.

Watt resigned effective October 9, 1983, and was replaced by "a God-fearing westerner, fourth-generation rancher, and a person I trust," President Reagan said. The successor, William P. Clark, was a longtime friend of Reagan's but, unlike Watt, apparently knew when to keep his mouth shut.

lawyer looked the other way as his agency became riddled with corruption. As people in the White House and elsewhere saw how inefficiently HUD really was run, they sent young, Republican appointees there to work. These people passed around government funding as if it were their own. The losers, of course, were the growing numbers of people without homes on big-city streets all across the country.

The HUD scandal and subsequent investigation spilled over into

A senior inspector of the New York City Department of Health holds up a discarded syringe on South Beach, Staten Island, in 1988. Medical waste, including vials of dried blood and hypodermic needles, was washed up onto the shore several times forcing New York City's beaches to close.

the first year of George Bush's presidency. Congressional investigators repeatedly sought sworn testimony from Pierce, who failed three times to appear when ordered to do so by the Government Operations Subcommittee. When he finally showed up, he refused to testify, citing the protection afforded him by the Fifth Amendment. Not since the Teapot Dome scandal during the Warren Harding administration in the 1920s had a cabinet member sought such protection from self-incrimination.

War on the EPA

Of all the agencies in the federal government, it seemed Ronald Reagan most disliked the Environmental Protection Agency. Why else did he appoint people to important EPA posts who were committed to developing every possible public and private acre of land? These appointees actually stood in the way of federally ordered cleanups and other chores overwhelmingly endorsed by the public. One such appointee was Rita Lavelle.

Lavelle was found guilty in 1983 of perjury and of obstructing a congressional inquiry. Dismissed earlier that year as head of the EPA's toxic-waste cleanup program, she had testified to Congress that she did not know about the dumping of hazardous wastes in a California disposal site by her former employer, Aerojet-General Corporation. Witnesses said she knew earlier of the illegal dumping and that she took official action only after talking to the company's legal counsel.

She also denied using the toxic-waste cleanup program for political purposes. Cleanup projects in California, Indiana, and Missouri had been slowed or speeded up because of their impact on elections. Lavelle's attorney indicated that she was a scapegoat. Others in the administration, he said, knew and approved of her actions. She served a short prison sentence.

Among those in the EPA for whom Lavelle covered may have been Anne Gorsuch Burford. Burford resigned amid congressional claims that she had taken Superfund money set aside for cleaning especially hazardous sites and had given part of it to polluters she knew so they could clean up their own messes with federal money. Congress also accused Burford and others of favoritism toward polluters, of mismanagement, and of compiling a "hit list" of dedicated environmentalists inside the EPA that they intended to fire.

John W. Hernandez, acting EPA administrator after Burford's resignation, resigned in March 1983 after it was learned that he had allowed Dow Chemical Company to tone down a report critical of their pollution of waterways. Hernandez also delayed cleanup of contamination in poor and minority neighborhoods, including lead in soil around grade schools. The senior official moved immediately from the EPA into a $245-a-day job with another government agency! In a move that amazed Republicans and Democrats alike, Ronald Reagan unsuccessfully attempted to appoint Burford to another EPA post in 1984.

That same year, Labor Secretary Raymond Donovan was indicted by a grand jury in New York. The jury accused Donovan of grand larceny and of falsifying business records while an executive with a large construction firm. Court documents showed that the money a subcontractor charged Donovan's company had been inflated to comply with federal regulations on minority-run businesses. Rumors had trailed the labor secretary since 1981, involving connections to organized crime and making illegal payoffs to public officials.

Donovan eventually stepped down, even though he was cleared of any wrongdoing. "Where do I go to regain my reputation?" he asked at a news conference. He was one of the unfortunate victims of eighties scandals and extremist politics who had a name. There were hundreds of other victims, in a Central American jungle, in a Harlem crack house, or in a Chicago housing project. They were unable to defend themselves, and their names went unrecorded.

ENVIRONMENT

For further information see primary source entries on pages

11: 1471-73; **12:** 1663-65, 1669-71, 1711-13

A hazardous waste team in protective suits is decontaminated outside a salvage store in Enterprise, Alabama. During the eighties there was increasing public concern over the dumping and storage of hazardous wastes.

CHAPTER 8
The Expansion of Technology

This wafer of silicon contains three hundred integrated circuits (or silicon chips). A diamond will be used to separate them from each other. The four vacant areas around the edge are for handling, and the five small rectangles that appear different from the chips are test areas used in the manufacturing process. Integrated circuits are the brains of computers. Their development throughout the seventies and eighties transformed computer technology.

By the time the principal got hold of a copy, the underground newspaper was all over the small-town Missouri high school. Like earlier efforts, this one had a strong, frequently off-color point of view. It made fun of several teachers, labeled the hardest-working students nerds, and advocated anarchy. But unlike similar fanzines, as the kids called them, this homemade magazine was carefully set in type and looked more professional than even the school newspaper. How, the principal worried, could a student afford such an extravagance?

Underground writers and editors didn't need much money by the mid-1980s — if they had access to personal computers and desktop publishing programs. Parents with such hardware and software encouraged their children to use them. Such fanzines, which most often were concerned with school rules or alternative music but could be used to spread hate and fanaticism, could be found in many teenagers' bedrooms. With a computer in the home, everyone could be a publisher — or, if part of a network connected by a device called a modem, the user could be a travel agent, stockbroker, or novelist. The person clicking merrily away on the keyboard also might be an intensely eighties kind of rebel that came to be known as a hacker.

Perhaps the decade's best-known hacker (one who uses a computer to connive, entertain, trick, or disrupt) was Robert T. Morris. The twenty-three-year-old Cornell University graduate student in computer science created a "virus" that spread through many military and academic computer systems nationwide. A total of six thousand computers, all of them connected to each other in one way or another, skidded to a halt as the program in which Morris had inserted his bug wiped out huge amounts of information.

Hackers didn't need to be whizzes in computer science. Since computers employed telephone lines to make connections, hackers needed only enough money to pay the long-distance bill each month, plus a computer and the modem that made the

phone line hookup possible. Hackers erased or altered hospital records, credit references, police data, bank accounts, defense secrets, and high school grades. In short, they were capable of changing anything on computerized records, given enough time to try numerous passwords to enter the systems.

The Home Computer

The first commercially available home computer, the $397 Altair, was offered in the mid–1970s and had only enough memory to store about a paragraph of information. Ten years later, home computers were capable of storing hundreds of times that much on floppy disks. As of 1985, portable laptop computers represented only $25 million in sales. But by 1989, sales of the small but mighty laptop machines exceeded $6.4 billion. By the end of 1990, there were about twenty-five million personal computers in American businesses alone. Clearly, the 1980s were the decade of the personal, mobile, and high-powered computer.

As time passed, software (the programs used to run computers) became more important and more of an

William Gates.

Bill Gates was in such a hurry to find out about personal computers that he dropped out of Harvard after being there just one year. The boyish young man with the big glasses and restless mop of hair soon created a programming language for one of the first personal computers, or PCs. He may not have known it then, but he was on schedule to be a multimillionaire.

Gates outraged fellow computer hackers by insisting that his software program be paid for rather than passed for free from one user to another. Why, Gates reasoned, should he give away something over which he had labored? It's hardly an exaggeration to state that his answer to that question aimed the entire personal computer business in a different direction in the late 1970s.

Gates soon began his own business, Microsoft Corporation. By the 1980s, Microsoft was selling all kinds of software, from word processing to spread sheets to flight simulators, intended for anyone who owned either an IBM computer, an IBM clone, or any computer in the Apple Macintosh series.

By 1990, Gates was the head of a $7 billion software empire with five thousand employees and forty different products. His success stems from the fact that IBM in 1980 chose Microsoft to supply the operating system for its own personal computers. This disk-operating system, or DOS, is now the means by which fifty million PCs operate. Every program that runs on an IBM or similar computer must work with Microsoft standards.

Gates has managed to irk many software companies by producing Microsoft programs that quickly take over the market due to the firm's reputation for success, service, and distribution. A hard-driving executive, he seems to thrive on, and get the best of, competition. He is the decade's best living proof that an individual with talent, intelligence, and drive can still succeed in the United States.

investment than hardware (the actual computers). By 1990, almost 40 percent of all personal computers were linked by telephone lines to other PCs in local networks. As new editions of software became available, it became more difficult to mysteriously lose work in a system or suffer other malfunctions. All of this technology rested, quite literally, on grains of sand.

The silicon chip, which made all this possible, was invented in 1959. About the size of a fingernail, the little chip of sand was covered with semiconductors to form an integrated circuit, that became the brain of a computer — or of something else. Eventually, everything from handheld games to automotive emissions systems to ballistic missiles were being run by these tiny forms of artificial intelligence. Santa Clara County, California, south of San Francisco, known as "Silicon Valley," grew dramatically as chip makers, programming wizards, and hardware manufacturers tried to respond to the incredible demand for their products.

Even though the rest of the country was mired in a grinding recession, "Silicon Valley" in the early 1980s was prosperous beyond anyone's dreams. People began to compare what was going on in Sunnyvale and other cities to the gold rush of 1849. Unfortunately, the prosperity did not last. At least twice during the decade, slumps in demand for various products resulted in thousands of layoffs, closed plants, and wild swings in the ability of local government to meet social and other demands. Even worse, the Japanese were beginning to produce their own chips in earnest. By the end of the decade, U.S. firms such as Motorola produced only about one-third of the world's semiconductors.

The *Challenger* Disaster

There may have been thousands of complex silicon chips on board the space shuttle *Challenger* on January 28, 1986, but a much simpler device would lead to tragedy. An O-ring, a floppy, rubberlike gasket the diameter of a quarter and big enough to encircle a redwood, grew brittle in the thirty-six-degree morning air on the Florida launch pad. Almost as soon as liftoff took place, the ring sealing shut the right booster rocket began to erode. Roaring flame from the booster blew very hot air against the craft's tank of liquid fuel. Seventy-three seconds after the 11:38 A.M. liftoff, *Challenger* exploded, falling in pieces into the Atlantic Ocean. National Aeronautic and Space Administration (NASA) employees and sightseers stood stunned as debris dropped from the sky for an hour. Seven astronauts died in the disaster.

The tragedy was compounded by the fact that a civilian was on board. Christa McAuliffe, who had taught social studies in Concord, New Hampshire, and who was an inspiration to students, was to be America's first teacher in space. The *Challenger* was an equal-opportunity killer — among the seven astronauts were another woman, a black man, and a Hawaiian man of Japanese heritage. The search for pieces of the craft went on for seven months, involving six thousand workers attempting to cover ninety-three thousand square miles of Florida's Atlantic Coast. Only about half of the material was recovered.

Initially, fingers were pointed at the manufacturer of the O-ring, Morton-Thiokol. But the Utah company had warned NASA well before

SPACE

For further information see primary source entries on pages

12: 1625-26, 1694-96

A Lockheed employee at the Kennedy Space Center watches the space shuttle Challenger *explode soon after takeoff from Cape Canaveral in January 1986. NASA had ignored a technical problem that was a threat to the safety of the crew in order to get the flight launched on schedule.*

the launch that material ensuring a perfect seal became brittle and unsafe in temperatures below fifty degrees. The very morning of the launch, Morton-Thiokol engineers pointed worriedly to icicles on the shuttle's support tower. Yet NASA decision makers ordered the flight to begin.

The error was human, of course, rather than mechanical. Buoyed by previous *Challenger* successes, NASA people assumed that no launch would ever fail. They also were under tremendous pressure to do things on time because they feared even the smallest glitch would result in a stingy Congress cutting their funds. As costs rose, NASA skimped on crew training, made do with inferior equipment, and put off spending money on improving safety. The results, seen live on television, shocked the country and the world. People who thought NASA was a waste of time and money grew in number.

Strategic Defense Initiative — "Star Wars"

The Strategic Defense Initiative (SDI) or, as it soon became known, "Star Wars," did not blow up, primarily because it never got off the ground. In fact, it may have been an idea Ronald Reagan himself retrieved from a movie in which he had once starred. At any rate, it was the ultimate in space-age defense and expense in the 1980s, and it bears a closer look.

The idea was simple: Construct a high-tech, defensive umbrella that would knock out missiles aimed at the United States (presumably launched by the Soviet Union) while they were in flight far out in space. This protection against ICBMs (intercontinental ballistic missiles) would have cost billions and taken years to construct, if at all possible, and it called for technology not yet invented. Despite its science-fiction quality, Reagan and his advisors bristled when reporters labeled it "Star Wars," after George Lucas's popular science-fiction movie.

There were also misgivings about the idea among some Reagan insiders. But others, mostly military men, formed a group supporting SDI. Long after Ronald Reagan was out of office, Star Wars supporters continued in vain to stump for more money for the system as the only foolproof way to control arms — at least the biggest and most frightening arms. It may have been only a coincidence that many of

The seven members of the Challenger *crew. Back row, left to right: El Onizuka, Christa McAuliffe, Greg Jarvis, Judy Resnik. Front row, left to right: Mike Smith, Dick Scobee, and Ron McNair.*

the suppliers of Star Wars technology were from Ronald Reagan's adopted home state, California, where much of the research money was being spent. By the end of the decade, the Star Wars idea — and the backing for it — was fading.

Advances in Medicine

Many strides were made in the various fields of medicine, though cancer death rates remained more or less constant throughout the period.

A gamma camera scans the head of a patient suffering from cancer. The camera is a device widely used in cancer management and detection. The color-coded image on the screen represents the radiation emitted by a tracer in the body. The radiation concentrates in the cancerous areas. Methods of detection and treatment for cancer improved throughout the decade, but the ultimate cure remained elusive.

In 1980, for example, 205.3 per 100,000 men died of cancer, with 163.6 women per 100,000 suffering the same fate. Ten years later, 221.3 men and 186 women per 100,000 were dying annually of cancer in its numerous forms. The disease was treated with surgery, with radiation, and with powerful medicines collectively known as chemotherapy. By the end of the decade, scientists knew certain people were predisposed to cancers, and they realized there would never be a single cure because there were so many kinds of cancer.

Nevertheless, signs were encouraging. Respiratory cancers were declining among the young because fewer of them used tobacco. There were many more cases of breast cancer being reported among older women, but that was due in part to careful self-examination and scheduled checkups. Digestive cancers also declined, probably because weight- and health-conscious Americans were eating lower-fat diets. Still, people diagnosed with cancers of the pancreas or the brain stood little chance of living longer than two years.

Prevention of another major killer, heart disease, showed good results. Death rates of males and females during the ten years in question declined about 20 and 10 percent, respectively. Besides increased knowledge of the benefits of diet and exercise, more heart-attack victims were surviving

A fast-food stand in Washington, D.C. Surveys in the 1980s concluded that cholesterol, which is found in meat and dairy products, is bad for the heart and arteries.

because of better emergency procedures. Physicians armed with everything from laser beams to space-age imaging machines could watch a patient's heartbeat on a screen as they injected dye and threaded tiny balloons into arteries to open clogged passageways. Heart-bypass surgery, unknown before the mid-1960s, had a mortality rate of approximately 1.5 percent by the mid-1980s.

A ten-year study concluded in 1984 showed that consumption of cholesterol, a substance found in meat and dairy products, increased the chances of heart ailments among middle-aged men. The National Heart, Lung, and Blood Institute reported that a low-cholesterol diet, leaning toward fruit, vegetables, bread, and pasta, and away from steak, cheeseburgers, french fries, and ice cream, could reduce the heart-disease risk by an estimated 50 percent. For those whose bodies failed to eliminate the cholesterol already there, a Merck & Co. preventive pill called Mevacor became available by prescription late in the decade.

Embryo Technology and Medical Costs Advance

The first baby produced from a frozen embryo was born in 1984. The baby was born in Australia, where the embryo had been implanted in the mother to allow her to have a child. Soon afterward, two California brothers told The *Wall Street Journal* that they would begin performing embryo transplants commercially. The surgeon and the biomedical engineer, good capitalists, estimated that they could treat as many as fifty thousand women annually, at a price of $4,000 to $7,000

per attempt. An opponent called the venture "a low-water mark for the free-enterprise system."

Prices for other medical care skyrocketed during the decade. In an attempt to hold down costs, health maintenance organizations, or HMOs, became more popular. They cut medical care by more than 25 percent, a 1984 study showed, by offering prepaid, group-practice health plans. There were three hundred HMOs that year, serving 12.5 million persons. HMO members were found to have 40 percent fewer hospital admissions and days in the hospital than did fee-for-service patients. Among other things, this meant that HMO users were more likely to go for less expensive preventive care, a hopeful sign. However, more recent looks at HMOs showed less optimistic figures.

Medical Failures and Dissension

Unfortunately, in its haste to make mankind immortal, the medical community sometimes neglected the basics. Autopsies studied in mid-1983 showed that the deaths of hundreds of patients could have been prevented by correct diagnosis. In 10 percent of cases, proper diagnosis and treatment would have prolonged patients' lives. In 12 percent of cases, diagnoses were incorrect. The study showed there was too much reliance by doctors on computerized equipment and not enough attention paid to human training and experience — hands-on medicine.

The downside of modern technology took many other forms. A contraceptive named the Dalkon Shield caused some women to become less fertile, even after use was

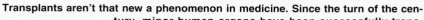

Robert Jarvik.

Transplants aren't that new a phenomenon in medicine. Since the turn of the century, minor human organs have been successfully transplanted. Yet few people prior to the 1980s attempted a heart transplant and fewer still succeeded when they tried. Physician Robert Jarvik decided the time had come to create an artificial heart.

Jarvik, born in Michigan in 1946, became a doctor and, in Utah, a teacher and researcher at an experimental laboratory. He secured a patent on a complete artificial human heart, powered by electrohydraulic energy. The first person to be fitted with the artificial polyurethane heart, appropriately enough, was a doctor himself. Dentist Barney Clark, who suffered from incurable heart disease, was given the Jarvik heart in 1982. He lived for 112 days.

It is difficult to separate one man from the other. Jarvik contributed skill and intensity to the first surgery, and Clark sacrificed his life, which would have ended much more quickly due to the inoperable disease of his own failing heart. Clark knew he faced immense odds; his participation was done on behalf of his fellow man. Others soon emulated Dr. Jarvik, who was honored with a number of awards.

discontinued. The intrauterine device (or IUD) was designed by A. H. Robins Co. In a related kind of problem, Procter & Gamble's Rely tampons had caused the sometimes fatal toxic-shock syndrome in more than a hundred American women. Numerous damage suits were filed against both companies by the victims or their next of kin, and feminists argued that products for use by men would have been more carefully tested.

Other disagreements based on politics or ideology conspired to make medicine a less-than-ideal profession. The National Institutes of Health and other major grant-giving organizations found themselves under pressure from special-interest groups. There were groups that did not want a cent spent on AIDS, groups that wanted every cent spent on AIDS, and groups that chided givers for neglecting breast cancer or ovarian cancer or other women's diseases. Childhood cancer, for example, totals only about eight thousand cases a year, nationwide. But because children are involved, a huge percentage of all cancer funds are earmarked for such research.

In a display of unanimity, U.S. religious leaders in 1983 asked Congress to limit genetic research and to ban genetic engineering. The Jewish, Protestant, and Roman Catholic leaders did not want anyone claiming the right "to make decisions on behalf of the rest of the species alive today or for future generations." In other words, no one should be involved with "improving" the human race. The clerics were opposed to the creation of human life, but endorsed repairing physical defects in individuals.

The religious leaders had good reason to make the pronouncement. In 1983, scientists working in the U.S. and in Belgium successfully transferred the gene from a bacterium into plant cells, where the gene functioned normally. These separate efforts struck many as being painfully close to creation. If laboratory wizards could move living material into a plant, what else might they do? Mental images of people creating humans (or worse, half human-half plant) frightened those who thought about it. Small wonder that scientists who were engaged in extraterrestrial work gained more attention. They were only dabbling with the universe.

Studying the Heavens

The Big Bang theory of the origin of the universe was well known and widely accepted by the 1980s. The theory held that some fifteen billion years ago, the universe was a solid mass. An explosion of unimaginable power blew apart the mass, forming stars, planets, and life as we know it. Probes by various satellites equipped with telescopes and other devices tended to reinforce this theory.

Equally exciting, physicists working on Earth were delving into the tiny building blocks of matter. They believed that every atom held a clue that would confirm how the universe got its start.

To conduct the research, scientists lobbied for and won approval of a superconducting supercollider, to be built south of Dallas, around Waxahachie, Texas. The project consisted of a circular, underground tunnel, fifty-four miles in circumference, where tiny bits of matter traveling in opposite directions would collide at speeds approaching the speed of light. The collision would give off the kind of power seen when the Big Bang took place, but since such small fragments were involved it would be more manageable. Smaller tunnels already were in place in Switzerland and Illinois. But the Waxahachie project would dwarf them all.

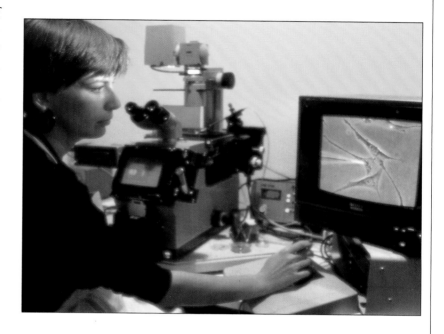

The accelerator, as it was called, would tell scientists what the universe was made of and what forces bind matter together. The collision of tiny particles would create different kinds of particles not seen in fifteen billion years! Completion of the project was predicted by the year 2000 at a cost of as much as $8 billion. Arguing for the project, U.S. scientists said it would keep the country ahead in particle-physics research. Failure to build the supercollider, scientists claimed, would result in American physicists going to Europe to do their research.

The understanding that might be gained from all this was seen by many as not worth the price tag. Cynics argued that the supercollider was being built in Texas because President Bush

Genetic research and engineering posed many ethical dilemmas in the 1980s. Here, a scientist introduces a corrective gene into a human white blood cell. The whole process can be seen on the computer screen as it happens.

was a Texan. A groundswell indicating that the money would be better spent on poverty or education ended the project before it got fully under way in the early 1990s.

Making Life Easier

Back above ground, technology was making lives easier as it prolonged them. Automobiles were first equipped with air bags, a restraint system much more effective in a front-end collision than seat belts alone. Packed into the center of steering wheels, air bags were activated as a collision took place, cushioning the body of the driver as it was hurled forward.

Research continued on vitamins and minerals in the human diet, and it was soon learned that they were of universal benefit, and that vitamins such as B and E could actually prolong life. The medical community also joined much of the public in urging research into the possible benefits of herbal medicines. Physicians admitted that they were not thoroughly trained in this field of medicine.

Sudden infant death syndrome (or SIDS), which killed hundreds of babies each year, was diagnosed and defeated in some cases with an electronic device. This sounded an alarm that woke parents whenever a child assumed a position that could cut off its breath.

In all, there were advances on many scientific fronts. Trouble was, the average American believed scientists and physicians sometimes intruded into areas best left to God, nature, or blind chance. The dying could be kept technically alive for long periods of time, leading many people to change their wills to prevent such action. Cynics joined the chorus, wondering why the world needed exotic gene therapy when it had failed to cure the common cold. The scientific community may have made some wonderful strides during the 1980s, but for the average American, they were as remote as ever.

This image of the planet Saturn was taken by the Voyager 1 *spacecraft at a distance of twenty-one million miles. The picture has been color enhanced by NASA to increase clarity. Three separate pictures, taken through ultraviolet, green, and violet filters, were used to construct this composite picture.*

CHAPTER 9
Everyday People

The middle-aged man of Hmong descent watched his youngest child trudge off through the Wisconsin winter to public school. What a contrast, he thought, between my life and hers. The father was born in the hilly jungles of Laos, half a world away from the upper Midwest. He had not ridden in or even seen a car, much less a telephone or a television set, until well into adulthood. Now, in the early 1980s, being in Wisconsin was as strange to him as being on the moon. My life is over, he concluded sadly, before realizing that the life of his daughter was only just beginning.

This Laotian-American was one of thousands of people resettled in the United States in the wake of the war in Vietnam. Similarly, immigrants from Africa, Central and South America, the Caribbean, Europe, and other parts of Asia waited for their chance to become citizens. By the end of the decade, about 30 million American residents of the total of 248 million spoke something other than English in their homes. Approximately 12 percent of the total population was black and 9 percent Hispanic. Females out-numbered males by about 6 million and only 55 percent of the nation's 91 million households were maintained by married couples.

Ten thousand people, mostly Hispanics, take part in a naturalization ceremony in the Orange Bowl, Miami, Florida, in September 1984. Miami is officially a bilingual city.

A Divided Society

IMMIGRATION

For further information
see primary source entries
on pages

11: 1454-60, 1484-85,
1490-91, 1514-16;
12: 1696-98, 1715-17

*Two Vietnamese women
haggle over the price of
fish in the Michoud area
of New Orleans, a
stronghold for Vietnamese
refugees.*

U.S. society was becoming more layered than a wedding cake. Shortly after World War II, the middle class encompassed everyone from the school janitor and his store-clerk wife to the divorce lawyer and her English professor husband. But that rich stew, which had cooked along contentedly in white, mainstream America, began to separate in the 1980s. More and more blue-collar workers, their jobs withering away, were sinking to the lowest layers of the middle class — or into a frightening area well below, known as the working poor. In fact, the U.S. Department of Labor, in a 1983 report, stated that an astonishing 20 percent of factory workers had been unemployed for at least some portion of the previous twelve months.

Blacks and Hispanics, less educated than whites, were the last to be hired and the first to be fired. In the roller-coaster economy, hirings and firings took place with alarming frequency. In Chicago, for example, when a new, luxury hotel advertised for help in 1989, more than four thousand people attempted to apply for jobs. Most of these unemployed yet willing people were minorities.

Hispanics, living disproportionately in fast-growing states such as California, Florida, and Texas, found government services stretched by Reagan administration cutbacks and by the avalanche of people in these areas. "Any gains that had been made were frozen as of 1980," said a political science professor of Hispanic heritage who taught at a college near the

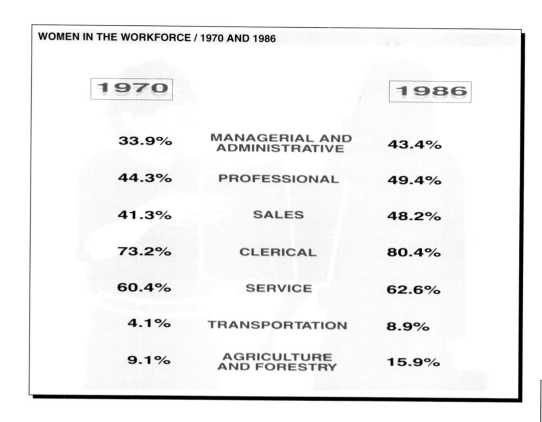

WOMEN IN THE WORKFORCE / 1970 AND 1986

1970		1986
33.9%	MANAGERIAL AND ADMINISTRATIVE	43.4%
44.3%	PROFESSIONAL	49.4%
41.3%	SALES	48.2%
73.2%	CLERICAL	80.4%
60.4%	SERVICE	62.6%
4.1%	TRANSPORTATION	8.9%
9.1%	AGRICULTURE AND FORESTRY	15.9%

In most occupations, women were a greater percentage of the workforce in 1986 than they had been in 1970. The greatest increases were in managerial and professional jobs, and in outdoor occupations. In less skilled jobs, percentages remained much the same. In 1970, women already made up more than half the workforce in clerical and service jobs.

Mexican border in Texas. In the prosperous Silicon Valley area of northern California, 50 percent of Hispanic students were dropping out of high school before graduation. Among eighteen- and nineteen-year-olds in a nationwide study, only 55 percent of Hispanics had completed high school. The future was not promising.

It looked even more bleak for African-Americans. Blacks in 1980s America saw the fabric of their lives torn by drugs, violence, and the disintegration of the family. The total number of poor Americans averaged about 13 percent throughout the decade, and of those thirty million Americans, a large number were both black and female. In fact, more than 30 percent of all African-Americans, or nine million of twenty-seven million, were classified as poor. Half of these poor were found in households headed by a woman. Generous media coverage of positive events in black communities could not hide the fact that most inner cities were black ghettos and those ghettos were hellish places in which to live.

Women had to settle for small victories. The U.S. Supreme Court ruled in 1981 that a woman could sue an employer over comparable worth. In other words, if she did the same kind of work and was equally qualified, she should be paid the same as a man. Sandra Day O'Connor joined the high court that same year, and two years later Astronaut Sally Ride explored space. Geraldine Ferraro accepted the Democratic vice presidential nomination in 1984, and a California court upheld the idea of granting maternity leave exclusively to women. An area of common ground between feminist and conservative women was pornog-

"We are passing from one generation to another a group of people who are hopelessly locked into a permanent underclass."

Congressman
Louis Stokes

raphy. Feminists hated it because they believed it incited violence against women. Conservatives simply found it degrading to portray humans in sexually explicit ways.

Meanwhile, there were new layers of the middle class who kept a safe distance from any ghetto. These included yuppies (young, urban professionals), dinks (double income, no kids), and a host of other acronyms that were dehumanizing but sometimes painfully accurate. They most often covered white men and women, between college and the age of forty, who dressed well, lived in expensive apartments, drove snazzy foreign cars, were somewhat well read, got the right amount of exercise, and worked in middle-management, banking, law, or high-technology positions.

They annoyed the rest of the population in different ways. Older and less affluent Americans considered them ostentatious. Cars such as BMWs became symbols of excess to people who were trying to patch together aging Chevys or Fords. Younger and less affluent American teenagers and college kids resented the fact that a yuppie could afford to buy dozens of compact discs in a single visit to a music store. On college campuses, "Die yuppy scum!" became a popular bumper sticker. But there were many collegians eagerly awaiting their chance to become urban and professional, too.

Many people saw money as power. Consequently, young executives consumed "power lunches" while wearing fashionable "power suits," oozing the "power look." Labels crept from the inside to the outside of clothes, as designer fashions boosted egos and fattened the cash registers of swank stores. The trend broadened as everything from T-shirts to blue jeans to tennis shoes sported distinctive logos — the swoosh of Nike, the red tab of Levi Strauss, the intricate initialing of Chanel, the roguish lettering and eagle symbol of Harley-Davidson.

Opiates of the Masses

If any such upwardly mobile people were vulnerable, it was in the area of drug abuse. For hundreds of

The yuppie was a 1980s invention — the word described affluent young people, sporting "power suits" and expensive cars and working in high-paying jobs such as finance, law, and management.

Barbara Harris.

Barbara Harris became a bishop of the Episcopal diocese of Massachusetts in February 1989. Naming the African-American woman to the position was a radical departure from the two thousand-year tradition of male-only apostles in the Episcopal church.

Rev. Harris was born in Philadelphia, grew up Episcopalian, and graduated from a girls' high school. She attended a journalism school and then joined a public relations firm that specialized in helping corporations reach African-American consumers. Simultaneously, she spent spare moments in the civil rights cause, participating in Martin Luther King's historic 1965 march from Selma to Montgomery, Alabama. She became increasingly active in social causes, feeding the poor and ministering to prisoners. In 1974, she was ordained an Episcopal priest.

Rev. Harris left her position as a senior consultant with a petroleum company to devote full time to her priestly duties in a Philadelphia suburb. She became head of the Episcopal Publishing Company, where she wrote a column criticizing church teachings and practices that she felt discriminated against women, homosexuals, and minorities. In 1987, a majority of American Episcopalian bishops decided that it was all right for a woman to serve as a bishop, and the stage was set for Harris.

The vote took place on September 24, 1988. Afterward, Episcopalians, Roman Catholics, and others spoke out against having a female bishop, indicating that the Episcopal church, which had served as a bridge between Catholic and Protestant faiths, was no longer suitable. Others condemned Harris's consistent activism. She was called "pro-Marxist," and even "pro-terrorist." Some church members questioned her lack of a seminary or theological degree. Harris was not welcome in several churches in her new Massachusetts diocese.

Small and with a voice that reminds some of actress Katherine Hepburn, Rev. Harris has emphasized prison ministry while consenting not to appear at Episcopal churches that might find her presence painful. In sum, she represents one of several new paths open to women in the eighties.

thousands of them, cocaine kept them buoyant. Many consumed even more of the illegal substance than their large incomes could support. Parties in fancy condominiums or co-ops often degenerated into "doing toots," sniffing powdered coke off an expensive coffee table through a rolled-up $100 bill. Like their less fortunate inner-city counterparts, these users supported a vast, illegal, international cartel while they toyed with their lives. Many found cocaine a habit they could never kick.

Despite the many alarms, cocaine was a relatively minor killer. A report issued in 1988 by the National Institute on Drug Abuse showed that most drug-related deaths each year were caused by tobacco — a total of 346,000. Alcohol was responsible for 125,000 fatalities, followed by a combination of drugs and alcohol that killed four thousand. Also responsible for four thousand deaths each year were either heroin or morphine. Cocaine killed two thousand people annually, with marijuana judged responsible for seventy-five deaths. Obviously, tobacco and alcohol were widespread, subtle killers of much more importance than any illegal substance.

Not all yuppies were obsessed with cocaine. In increasing numbers, young urban professionals and other Americans with and without labels were becoming religious. Much of this new-found emphasis on Christianity came directly from television. The number of Christian ministries in the U.S. that broadcast regularly on TV climbed from twenty-five in 1978 to 336 in 1989. Evangelical Christians developed sophisticated communications systems that resulted in much more influence than the older, more established churches. Mainline Protestants, such as Methodists and Presbyterians, watched as younger members in particular were lured away.

Some broadcasters traced their roots to the Pentecostal movement early in this century. Groups of people in Kansas and in California, angry that Methodist evangelism (recruiting) had lost fervor, began holding their own services. These meetings were marked by thundering hymns, moving sermons delivered by hypnotic leaders, and by baptism. They also sometimes featured people talking gibberish (called speaking in tongues) and faith healing. One small sect gained notoriety by using poisonous snakes in its services! Long dismissed as low-class "Holy Rollers," these people were largely ignored until television thrust them into the nation's living rooms.

Televangelism

Televangelists such as Jim Bakker, Jerry Falwell, Pat Robertson, and Jimmy Swaggart successfully recruited thousands. Bakker and Swaggart were Pentecostalists, Falwell was a Fundamentalist (interpreting the Bible literally). Robertson was a Charismatic Christian, a movement that included all denominations. Their messages were conservative, and their ministries became well financed as they successfully sought donations. Through it all, they were encouraged by no less than Ronald Reagan.

Not a churchgoer himself, Reagan crusaded for the conservative themes that evangelists loved, such as outlawing abortion and stamping out pornography. With such endorsements, religious broadcasters reached about one-quarter of the viewing public. Jerry Falwell replaced the more-established evangelical Billy Graham as the unofficial chaplain of the Republican White House.

Obviously, televangelism's messages would have been lost without a receptive audience. There was one. The most likely convert to this new religion was a troubled lower-middle-class adult who was easily led and who was baffled by modern technology and the increasing complexity of society. Televangelists told Americans it was all right to make money and that it was OK to lean more on faith and less on serving one's fellow humans. Access to the airwaves became easy for the televangelists when, in the late seventies, the Federal Communications Commission decided that religious programming fulfilled a television station's public-service duties.

There's no telling how far the

Jim Bakker.

Jim Bakker and his wife, Tammy Faye, came from blue-collar backgrounds in Michigan. Bakker attended divinity school in Minnesota, and the two hit the road in a soul-saving ministry. In time, Bakker learned of the power of televised preaching and gathered a sizeable following, supported by $4 million a month in donations. The Bakkers traveled by private jet and owned six homes.

The televangelist's troubles began in 1980, when he had an affair with a Long Island church secretary named Jessica Hahn. Bakker paid Hahn more than $250,000 to keep her mouth shut about their affair, but she went public anyway.

Bakker was tried and then sentenced in October 1989 to forty-five years in prison and fined $500,000. He had been found guilty of all twenty-four counts brought against him for fraud and conspiracy. The charges involved his misuse of church funds, which are not taxable when used honestly and as intended. Evidence of further excesses included Bakker's purchase of an air-conditioned doghouse! The trial took place in Charlotte, North Carolina, a Bible Belt city that contained hundreds of people who had followed and believed in Bakker's televised ministry. For them he put on a special final performance.

He blamed his downfall on the devil, on greedy employees, on fellow televangelist Jerry Falwell, and, of course, on Jessica Hahn. Tammy Faye offered up a tearful hymn to the microphones and the cameras before her husband was led away by federal marshals. Bakker's attorneys appealed his sentence without success, and he remains behind bars.

It's certainly easy to laugh at Jim Bakker and his now former wife. Yet it should be remembered that they shattered the beliefs of many God-fearing citizens who sent the Bakkers money when it may not have been easy to do so. It's equally important to recall that both were at one time deeply religious and powerful evangelical personalities.

various televised movements would have gone had not sin reared its ugly head. Jim Bakker admitted having sexual relations outside his marriage and was imprisoned for spending tax-exempt church money on himself. Jimmy Swaggart admitted to dealing with prostitutes, adding to his woes with a tear-stained, theatrical confession before leaving the airwaves. Pat Robertson ran unsuccessfully as a Republican candidate for president in 1988. His chances were dashed after it was learned that Robertson's father used his influence to save the then-young marine from combat in Korea.

Falwell had created a political organization called the Moral Majority, which worked to elect conservative Christians. Falwell was the most successful and least tainted of all the televangelists, having rallied Moral Majority members to defeat several Democratic U.S. senators and congressmen with whom he disagreed. He departed from that organization to return to his Virginia congregation, and also started a college.

An older and more traditional minister, Oral Roberts, told followers in 1987 that "God could call Oral home in March" unless $4.5 million was given to prop up his Oklahoma-based religious and medical college. Reverend Donald Wildmon, upset with what he saw as anti-Christian and profane television programming, operated the Mississippi-based American Family Association, threatening to boycott the sponsors of "obscene" shows.

From Evangelism to the New Age

Evangelicals weren't always predictable. Representatives meeting in California in 1984 endorsed the peace movement and the drive for nuclear disarmament. The respected Gallup Poll that same year showed that 60 percent of evangelicals questioned favored an immediate and verifiable nuclear freeze. America's thirty million evangelicals differed little from mainline religions or the general public on the issue.

The Roman Catholic leadership in America condemned the arms race, too. American Catholicism was doing well. There were more than fifty-five million Catholics, making it by far the largest Christian church. American Catholicism differed from the parent church in several areas, especially on matters of birth control, divorce, and social activism. Pope John Paul II admonished U.S. bishops in 1983 to adhere more closely to church teachings on sex and marriage and to reinforce the belief that women should not participate in the Mass. Catholic bishops in the U.S. issued letters renouncing the use of force in Central America, advocating a ban on nuclear weapons, and beginning a study on the role of women. They saw no

Emmett White, a medicine man of the Pima tribe, presents Pope John Paul II with an eagle feather in Phoenix, Arizona, during the 1987 papal visit to the U.S. The eagle is sacred in many American Indian cultures, and its feathers are awarded for acts of courage or great accomplishment.

A paramedic checks a child for wounds as the mother cries outside the McDonald's restaurant in San Ysidro, California, where James Oliver Huberty gunned down and killed twenty-two people.

irony in the fact that an all-male group would conduct this study.

At the other end of the spectrum, New Age religions gained adherents. Any of several religions recently conceived in California, the New Age could feature use of crystals in healing and communicating or channeling with persons who lived long ago. Several leaders, male and female, held sessions that explored whether a participant might have been someone else in a previous life. Neither numerous nor strictly organized, New Agers were interested in everything from Oriental religions to the beliefs of American Indians. They were alternatively spoofed and taken seriously by Hollywood and by creators of TV comedies and dramas.

Self-Healing and Failure to Cope

Those who had problems and who weren't religious could turn to a bewildering number of self-help groups for a wide variety of issues. There were disorders connected to marriage and divorce, to romance and sex, to parenthood, to childhood, and to various addictions. This generation, it was said, suffered from the lost ideals of youth. Baby boomers, Americans born between 1946 and 1958, were in charge and were shocked that they had at least as many troubles as their parents. Even people who took no comfort from money often needed to join groups; there was even a self-help group for lottery winners! In all such regular gatherings, people would pour out their souls and then go home, apparently feeling better for listening to others' problems and for having someone they could talk to.

Some Americans turned to religion, others looked inward, and still others simply failed, taking their failure to cope out on society. One, James Oliver Huberty, dismissed from his job as a security guard, committed one of the largest mass murders in U.S. history on July 18, 1984, when he opened fire on diners inside a McDonald's restaurant in San Ysidro, California, killing twenty-two. The hideous spree lasted seventy-seven minutes before the gunman was killed by a sharpshooter.

Huberty's motivations may never be known, but his pattern is familiar. A welder in Ohio, he was laid off in 1982 and lost another job before moving his family to California. But he could find only low-paying jobs, and his resentment grew as he collected firearms for his last deadly act. Similar slaughters took place with unsettling regularity in many parts of the country.

Public Schools in Crisis

Almost as disturbing was a federal commission's 1983 study that severely criticized the quality of American education and called for improvements in the nation's schools. Continued neglect, they said, would threaten the foundations of the country. Established in 1981, the National Commission on Excellence in Education issued a report it titled, "A Nation at Risk: the Imperative for Educational Reform." It recommended that:

● High schools require students to study English, mathematics, science, social studies, and computer science, and to place added emphasis on foreign languages.

● Schools begin longer workdays and increase the school year from the present 180 to as many as 220 days each year. The recommendations also said students should spend more time doing their homework.

● Teachers' pay be directly connected to merit. In other words,

financial incentives should be used to make the teaching profession more attractive to the very best college graduates to lure them into a profession they might not otherwise consider.

● Colleges and universities adopt higher admissions standards.

These and other recommendations were necessary, commissioners believed, to combat the "rising tide of mediocrity" that was sweeping America's schools. Compared to children in other countries, American children had inferior skills — and those skills were getting worse. Research showed that scores on college admissions tests had declined steadily for twenty years and that 13 percent of all seventeen-year-old American high school students were functionally illiterate. Students and parents were disinterested in education, the report concluded.

The findings were interpreted very differently by different people. Ronald Reagan, whose biggest previous concern with education involved prayer in schools, believed it was a call to end "federal intrusion" into education. He pledged to dismantle the federal Department of Education. Secretary of Education Terrel Bell resigned in disgust in 1985 over the president's lack of interest in and funding of public education. Meanwhile, the National Education Association, the country's largest teachers' organization, called the commission's work important. The NEA, however, said the study was a call for the commitment of "billions" of federal dollars in order to improve matters.

Everyone agreed that schools were failing at their tasks. Chicago was accused of having the nation's worst public school system; the only

"The educational foundations of our society are presently being eroded by a rising tide of mediocrity that threatens our very future as a nation and a people."

The National Commission on Excellence in Education in *A Nation at Risk*, 1983

A classroom in "English on Wheels," in the Salinas Valley, California. This school traveled to the fields to teach English to Mexican migrant workers.

thing remarkable about the accusation was the small number of Chicagoans who disagreed with it. Repeatedly throughout the decade, kids were cornered in all parts of the country and asked questions that showed their ignorance of English, geography, history, and mathematics. Poor African-American children in particular were shortchanged as the population demanded local control — supporting local schools with local dollars. In poor school districts, the result was, of course, an inferior education.

"Not in My Backyard"

RACE

For further information
see primary source entries
on pages

11: 1460-64, 1474-75,
1504-05, 1518-19

An exchange of blows between a Ku Klux Klan supporter and an anti-KKK protester during a street demonstration in Atlanta, Georgia, in 1988.

Was America, after decades of liberal open-mindedness, also becoming a less tolerant place? It certainly seemed that way, as "NIMBY" — not in my backyard — became the favored acronym of many. In all-white Forsythe County, Georgia, outside Atlanta, hundreds of racists harassed twenty thousand marchers who were protesting the fact that no blacks had lived in the county since 1912. On the opposite coast, neighbors of a halfway house for former mental patients in Ventura, California, encircled their houses with six-foot fences. Both events took place in 1987. Skinheads, Ku Klux Klansmen, and survivalists worried authorities,

paticularly for their willingness to use violence to reach their goals.

But the decade was a breakthrough in two areas for more than eight million Vietnam-era veterans. A memorial dedicated to the fifty-seven thousand killed during that unpopular war was finally unveiled in Washington, D.C. The ebony wall with the name of every person who died quickly became the most-visited site in the nation's capital. Ground was broken for the project in 1982, and the dedication took place two years later. Meanwhile, a huge class-action suit (brought by one or more plaintiffs on behalf of a large group of people with a similar complaint) involving fifteen thousand Vietnam veterans was settled out of court. Seven chemical companies that had produced the

dioxin-based herbicide Agent Orange agreed to set up a $180 million fund to treat those who were exposed to the substance while serving in Vietnam. The settlement was reached only hours before a jury was to be chosen in the case, which centered on whether the herbicide had caused cancer and other maladies among the Vietnam veterans.

Homosexuality took one step forward and at least two steps back. Many Americans saw gay men not as the victims of the AIDS disease but its cause. Openly gay sections of major cities such as New York and San Francisco were avoided by people who feared the affliction. Some gays took courage from the adversity, telling parents and coworkers about their homosexuality. Families of people killed by AIDS and gays formed an activist alliance that gathered strength as it focused on finding a cure for the disease. But the armed forces continued to oust people such as Navy Commander Gerald M. Vanderwier, dismissed in 1983 for engaging in a homosexual act with a crewman on a ship he commanded.

About the Homeless

Los Angeles officials endlessly shuttled homeless residents from beneath viaducts and overpasses to camps and back in 1987. The endless prodding of these one thousand men, women, and children was only one manifestation of the problem. Homeless residents of major cities increased in number all during the decade. At its end, a Bureau of the Census survey indicated that an average of 178,828 persons were in homeless shelters, 23,383 were in emergency shelters,

and 10,447 were on the streets. New York led the unenviable list with the most homeless. Other cities with large numbers of homeless persons included Chicago, Los Angeles, San Francisco, and Washington, D.C.

A curious thing happened to the homeless at the end of the 80s: Many big-city people grew tired of their panhandling. Residents with social consciences bought vouchers that they

An elderly, homeless man in Detroit, Michigan, pours himself soup and tries to keep warm over a garbage can fire during a cold spell in January 1985.

> *"My program hasn't hurt anybody. No one has been thrown out in the snow to die."*
>
> Ronald Reagan, 1982

> *"We've had considerable information that people go to soup kitchens because the food is free .... That's easier than paying for it."*
>
> Attorney General Ed Meese

handed to homeless beggars. The tickets, unlike money, could be exchanged only for food. One ingenious person in New York City produced a special daily newspaper, *Street News*, that homeless residents could sell for seventy-five cents, thereby earning twenty-five cents per sale. Despite such efforts, occasional stories were reported of the homeless being set on fire or otherwise tormented and tortured.

Child Abuse and Teenage Violence

In contrast to its disregard for the homeless, the country became morbidly curious about child abuse. The media responded by giving readers more than they wanted to know about the subject. Typical was the case of Lisa Steinberg, a six-year-old living in New York City's Greenwich Village. Her lawyer father, Joel Steinberg, beat the child on a November day in 1987 until she was brain-dead. Three days after doctors unplugged life-support systems, she expired. The part of this sad story that outraged the nation was the fact that Steinberg had been reported repeatedly for beating his female companion and their two small children.

The Steinberg case and other evidences of nationwide child abuse put teachers on alert. One state, Missouri, passed a law that made a teacher liable if he or she failed to report the suspected beating of a child by a parent. Reports of abuse surged and then leveled off as people were shocked by various stories and came forward. Over zealous people sometimes turned in innocent fathers and mothers and boyfriends on the notion that abuse had occurred but that the victim had repressed all memory of it.

If young children were being carefully protected, their older siblings were being looked at with alarm, especially if they were African-American. Teenagers were involved in several instances of savagery that lingered in American memories. One was the vicious rape and beating of a white female jogger in New York City's Central Park by a group of black teens who attacked the young woman in a mindless episode of "wilding." Earlier in the decade, also in New York, Bernhard Goetz, a subway passenger, opened fire on several black teenagers who asked him for money and threatened him. Goetz was found innocent of assault and convicted of illegal gun possession.

Attacks on Social Activism

Social activism in the 1980s took several hits — the demise of the Equal Rights Amendment to the U.S. Constitution was no doubt the biggest. A total of thirty-five states of the thirty-eight required for ratification had passed the ERA. The amendment, endorsed by most women and many men, was despised by conservatives, and would have made sex discrimination illegal. There were other attacks on the activism of previous decades.

President Reagan endorsed allowing private schools to practice racial discrimination. Though the U.S. Supreme Court would later uphold the Internal Revenue Service's action not to give such schools tax-exempt status, the president favored the positions of two biased, white, fundamentalist schools in South Carolina.

In another case, approximately

seven hundred thousand young men had neglected to register for the military draft in 1982, but not many declined for moral or religious reasons. Among the few to confront the government, Christian pacifists, such as twenty-year-old Enton Eller, were ordered to register or face a term in prison. Eller was ordered to perform 250 hours of community service and was placed on probation for three years.

Except for an ongoing leak to the media from the president's National Security Council during Reagan's first term, there were few whistle blowers. People who reported evil doings in the government agencies or in businesses where they worked usually found themselves unemployed. Investigative journalism all but expired. It was replaced by "soft," publicity-oriented news as found in *People* magazine or in any of several pseudo-news shows such as "Entertainment Tonight" or "Inside Edition." None of the magazines or television entertainment reporting bore much relationship to the news — or to reality.

Jesse Jackson.

Few Americans have been as durably popular as Jesse Jackson. Born the son of a poor woman in Greenville, South Carolina, in 1941, Jackson burst on the scene in Chicago during the turbulent 1960s as a leader of African-Americans in that troubled city.

Jackson refused to endorse or participate in urban rioting, but he pointed out that uneven justice and deprivation had led African-Americans to disregard the law. A minister in the Baptist Church and a fiery speaker, Jackson became a member of the Southern Christian Leadership Conference and, in 1971, founded and became the director of Operation PUSH (People United to Save Humanity).

Throughout the 1970s and 1980s, Jackson urged black people to "put education in your brains, not dope in your veins" and to get involved in the political process. He followed his own advice, offering himself as a Democratic candidate for president prior to the 1984 and 1988 elections. He attracted attention during his first run and gained widespread backing during his second as the leader of what he termed the "Rainbow Coalition." People who backed Jackson in 1988 (he won an astonishing five primaries on Super Tuesday, the most active day in nationwide primary voting) were from all backgrounds and were all colors, hence the rainbow name. In both races for the Democratic nomination, traditional Democrats dismissed Jackson as a serious candidate, asking instead, "What does Jesse want?" trying to ferret out a hidden agenda.

Jackson wanted African-Americans and others on the lower rungs of the economic ladder not to be taken for granted when Democrats looked around for support. He despised the neglect of the poor, the young, and the disadvantaged by the Reagan administration and believed his candidacy to be a wake-up call for the Democratic party and for the country.

Jackson had his problems. Rumors floated about that he was a ladies' man or that he had some sort of secret agenda. But the religious activist gained widespread respect by winning the release of some U.S. citizens held hostage in the Mideast and in Cuba, and by speaking out when most Democrats were knuckling under to rich folks who were bankrolling Ronald Reagan and the Republican party.

CIVIL RIGHTS

For further information see primary source entries on pages

11: 1582-83; **12:** 1627-32, 1635-38, 1643-50, 1652-55

CHAPTER 10
The Bush Presidency

George Bush lacked sex appeal, and the presidential candidate's advisors had figures to prove it. In the spring of 1988, immediately after it became apparent that the vice president would win the Republican presidential nomination, Bush's staff commissioned a survey. It indicated that the candidate had significant support among male voters but was unpopular with women. What Bush needed, they believed, was a young and handsome vice presidential running mate who would woo female voters away from anyone the Democrats might nominate. The person chosen was Dan Quayle.

Quayle appeared to have all the credentials. He was handsome, which was all Bush advisors believed would be necessary to attract women voters.

He was conservative, which was important since the right wing of the Republican party had long been a bit suspicious of George Bush. And he was deeply involved in Republican politics as a U.S. senator from Indiana.

Quayle accepted the offer with enthusiasm, pointing out that he was a veteran campaigner, that he was a loving family man, and that his only obsession was golf, which he played very well every chance he got. He failed to report to Bush advisors that he had taken advantage of his parents' wealth and influence to gain admission to Indiana University's school of law. Nor did he point out that his law school grades were so underwhelming that he never allowed them to be made public. Most damaging, the Quayle family secretly managed, dur-

Dan Quayle, a young, relatively unknown senator from Indiana, was Bush's surprise choice for a running mate in 1988. Questions were raised why Quayle was chosen. Some surmised his image would attract female voters, while others felt Bush wanted a non-threatening presence as vice president.

Presidential candidates Republican George Bush and Democrat Michael Dukakis debate during the campaign in September 1988. Republican campaign managers tried again and again to blacken Dukakis's character in a particularly negative campaign.

In the end, Dukakis himself did not have a colorful enough personality to appeal to the American public.

ing the height of the Vietnam War, to find a safe spot for their son in the Indiana National Guard.

The less attractive aspects of Dan Quayle were quickly uncovered following the Republican convention. How could Republicans, those fierce guardians of the Pentagon budget, support a slate that included a draft dodger? Reporters took great delight in pointing out that Quayle's family backed the Vietnam War in its chain of newspapers while their son played weekend warrior. While Mrs. Bush impressed everyone as a motherly source of inspiration, Mrs. Quayle came across as a frequent meany. Amid serious talk of removing Bush's choice of a running mate, the GOP simply waited until the Democrats made their own kinds of mistakes. They did not have long to wait.

Michael Dukakis chose long-time Senator Lloyd Bentsen to be his vice presidential running mate. It looked to be a wise decision since Bentsen was somewhat conservative and from Texas, the home of George Bush,

whereas Dukakis was from Massachusetts. Dukakis's problem was that his honesty and forthrightness were unable to mask the fact that he came across as an emotionless person. During one of three debates between the Democratic and Republican candidates, the Massachusetts governor seemed almost frighteningly unconcerned over a question concerning the imagined rape of his wife.

Bentsen introduced the best line of the campaign in his debate with Quayle. The Republican compared his career to that of John F. Kennedy, and the lanky Bentsen swelled to his full height as he stared down the younger man. "I knew Jack Kennedy," he thundered. "And you are no Jack Kennedy."

Dirty Politics

Unfortunately for the Democrats, that was about as nasty as they could be. In contrast, Republican campaign managers devised several television ads

> *"I'm not a yuppie. I'm a senator."*
>
> Senator Dan Quayle

portraying Michael Dukakis as having made Boston Harbor a dumping ground for pollution and providing Massachusetts criminals with a revolving door that put them back out on the street immediately after their convictions. Even worse, GOP ad makers used the mug shot of a convicted black man, Willie Horton, in a blatantly racist ad that "proved" Dukakis allowed murderers to be set free at will. Dukakis hurt himself by failing to respond to these false allegations.

George Bush did not advance the various rumors made up to discredit his Democratic opponents, but he did little to stop them. Bush had come to national office as a middle-of-the-road Republican. However, he and his handlers correctly sensed the mood of the country and began to call Dukakis a liberal because they knew liberals were no longer in favor. Small wonder that Dukakis's wife, Kitty, attempted suicide and was hospitalized in 1989, after the campaign was over. Dukakis, a studious and colorless man, probably wondered why he ever accepted the Democratic nomination.

Ironically, the Democratic ticket

Michael Dukakis (right) is interviewed by ABC-TV's Ted Koppel.

Michael Dukakis.

The son of Greek immigrant parents, Michael Dukakis left Massachusetts while a very popular governor there to run for president in 1988. He probably wonders to this day if it all was worth it. . . .

A graduate of Harvard Law School after serving in the U.S. Army, Dukakis practiced law, successfully running as a Democrat for the governorship in 1975. Prior to that, from 1962 to 1970, he served in the Massachusetts House of Representatives. He held the governor's post until 1979, then was elected to the state's highest office again in 1983 and in 1987.

Dukakis gained a reputation as a very thrifty person. He bought his suits in a department store bargain basement, his snowblower was secondhand, and he drove an old Chevrolet to the governor's office each morning. He also was something of a television personality, serving as host for a local political news show called "The Advocates" from 1970 to 1973. He lectured at Harvard University and chaired several important committees made up of the nation's governors.

It wasn't enough, so he ran for president. Dukakis was at best a mediocre campaigner, and he began his run for federal office just as troubles began to mount in the state he had run. Massachusetts had reached the end of prosperity for its high-tech industries, resulting in high unemployment. Taxes remained high and housing was in short supply — two liabilities Democratic primary opponents and then George Bush and the Republicans delighted in bringing up in debates with the Democratic candidate.

Dukakis debated adequately with Bush, but he failed to understand or answer correctly a question about the hypothetical rape of his wife put to him by a reporter. His lack of emotion did not play well on national television. Nevertheless, he and running mate Lloyd Bentsen fared better in 1988 than did the Democrats four years earlier. They captured ten states and the District of Columbia.

The nominee's popularity declined rapidly in Massachusetts, where a late eighties recession was taking its toll. Events also took their toll on Dukakis's wife, Kitty, who abused alcohol and attempted suicide. Dukakis returned to teaching after his governmental duties ended.

probably would have been headed by Gary Hart, a U.S. senator from Colorado. But Hart confirmed rumors that circulated about him from the time he announced his intention to run for the presidency back in 1983. Washington insiders whispered that, like the Kennedys before him, Hart was a womanizer. Though he was a husband and father, that failed to curb his flirtations. Hart denied it all until a newspaper printed an accusation that he and a thirty-year-old sales representative named Donna Rice had spent a 1987 weekend in Florida on a yacht appropriately named *Monkey Business*. Hart sheepishly quit the race, then tried without success to run again at the last minute.

None of the candidates excited the average voter, which was probably why the Bush-Quayle ticket won with a narrower margin than did the Reagan-Bush duo in 1984. Republicans trooped faithfully to the polls, but some Democrats who had voted for Reagan in 1980 and 1984 returned to their own party. Officially, the GOP outpolled the Democrats 48.9 million votes to 41.8 million votes. The Dukakis-Bentsen ticket carried ten states and the District of Columbia. In all, just 50.1 percent of eligible voters bothered to go to the polls; it was the lowest percentage in U.S. history.

America in 1989

George Bush faced a country very different from the one he and Ronald Reagan encountered in 1980. Back then, monetary inflation and economic stagnation were the big worries. Beginning with his inauguration on January 20, 1989, Bush was confronted with a country that was strangling on the federal deficit created by Reagan. The two consecutive Reagan administrations had borrowed heavily, causing the amount of money the government owed — and interest it had to pay — to skyrocket. By 1989, the deficit was climbing at a rate of $12 billion a month. Stated another way, every American was paying $4

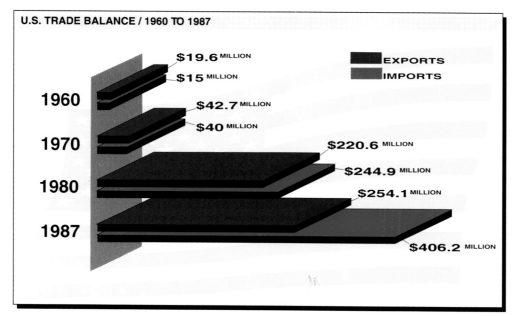

Both imports and exports increased through the seventies. During the eighties, however, imports began to outstrip exports, opening up a damaging trade deficit. By 1987, the deficit was out of control, severely weakening the nation's economy.

in interest every day on his or her share of the federal debt!

In a bipartisan report, former Presidents Jimmy Carter and Gerald Ford warned against borrowing from abroad to meet "the weekly need for more money." The future of the United States, they told the country, was "now in the hands of foreign investors." These foreigners included Japanese, Europeans, and Middle Easterners. The cost of the defense spending spree between 1980 and 1988 without a corresponding tax hike was coming home to roost on the shoulders of the forty-first president.

The new leader had other problems. Poverty was rampant and still growing, with thirty-three million Americans considered poor. Children born in the U.S. were much more likely to be part of a poverty-stricken family than their counterparts in several European countries or Canada. An estimated thirty-seven million children

and adults had no health insurance. Children in a dozen other countries were more likely to survive the trauma of birth than in the U.S., while their older brothers and sisters were more likely to complete high school or its equivalent. American kids were quite likely to be functionally illiterate and they were unable to fill out a simple job application.

Schools were dismal and getting worse. Suburban school districts, with plenty of money and not many kids, were less inclined than ever to support inner-city districts, where there were all too many children and too little money. The quality of teaching seemed to be in decline, too, even though class sizes were smaller than twenty years before. An international survey, paid for by the National Science Foundation, discovered in 1989 that compared to schoolchildren from several European and Asian nations, America's kids finished dead last in mathematics and were among the lowest in science. With the nation aging, the growing number of retirees often voted down referenda that would pay for more and better education, which they personally could not benefit from. Colleges were accused of abandoning the foundations of learning for courses the students wanted — studies of comic books, rock 'n' roll or vague religions.

Several other black clouds blew back and forth by the time George Bush settled into the Oval Office. The Soviet Union was all but history, though this third-world country with its first-world armaments would continue to convulse well into the decade that followed. Ethnic Russians seemed amenable to destroying offensive weapons, but Ukrainians and other groups vowed to hold onto their armaments. While places such as

George Bush became a member of the U.S. House of Representatives in 1966 and served in several important posts abroad and in the CIA before campaigning for the presidency and becoming vice president in 1980.

southeast Asia still experienced prosperity, much of Africa remained mired in bad government, starving people, and warring bandits.

At home, greed petered out as the real-estate market flattened, specialty-store sales declined, the junk-bond market collapsed, and financial institutions tightened credit restrictions. George Bush and Dan Quayle looked back at the Reagan years, liked what they saw, and surrounded themselves with people who reminded everyone of the earlier eighties, such as former New Hampshire Governor John Sununu. He advocated shutting down Congress by having the White House neither initiate nor act on any legislation. Unfortunately, Sununu also advocated using military jets and limousines to take him to stamp-collecting conventions. Confronted by the press in the spring of 1991 about personal trips at government expense, he resigned in December, 1991. In a move that could occur only in America, Sununu became a television talk-show regular in 1992.

Tall and angular, George Herbert Walker Bush looked and acted perpetually uncomfortable. Born in 1924 and the son of a wealthy U.S. senator from Connecticut, Bush served with honor in World War II as a U.S. Navy pilot. He was chauffeured to college — Yale University — before moving to Texas in the late 1940s and founding an oil company with his father's money.

Bush ran unsuccessfully for the U.S. Senate in 1964 before being elected to the U.S. House of Representatives in 1966 and 1968. He lost another Senate bid in 1970 and was named in the 1970s to important posts in the United Nations, in China, and in the CIA, where he served two years as that agency's director. After losing a bid for the Republican nomination in 1980, he was elected Ronald Reagan's vice president. For eight years, Bush served faithfully under the former movie star.

Sadly, the Bush administration's ethics proved conclusively to be not much better than its predecessors. In 1989, arrangements were made through the Atlanta branch of an Italian bank to send $3 billion to Saddam Hussein's government in Iraq. When long-time Democratic Congressman Henry Gonzalez of Texas began asking questions about the transaction, he was told by Attorney General Richard Thornburgh that national security was involved. Efforts by Bush aides to cut a deal with Gonzalez failed, resulting in the "Iraqgate" scandal.

It appears that U.S. government money helped Saddam Hussein pay for chemical and nuclear weapons, despite the administration's insistence that the money was for agricultural and other harmless purposes. Furthermore, Bush's foreign-policy experts continued to press for aid to Hussein even after other branches of government warned them of the Iraqi leader's slaughter of ethnic Kurds in Iraq and of his desire to take over neighboring Kuwait. In other words, the little bank in Atlanta had been helping to arm Iraq! The federal probe of the entire matter continued well into the 1990s.

Bush whined about the matter when questioned by reporters. "Why the Congress keeps spending the taxpayers' monies on these witch hunts, I do not know," he said. "I'm a little sick of it." Though he had asked voters in 1988 "to make kinder the face of

Henry B. Gonzalez. (1914-1998)

Was there no one in government worth idolizing in the 1980s? Yes, there was. Henry Gonzalez, longtime member of the U.S. House of Representatives and chairman of the House Banking, Finance, and Urban Affairs Committee, survived attacks on his sanity and his patriotism in order to get to the bottom of more than one scandal.

He grew up in a bilingual home in San Antonio. Gonzalez served as a censor with Army and Navy intelligence in World War II and earned degrees in law from St. Mary's University and the University of Texas.

He worked in his father's translating business and did everything from serving as a probation officer to running San Antonio's housing authority before being elected to the House of Representatives from San Antonio in 1961. He was repeatedly reelected, always as a progressive Democrat from the primarily Hispanic-American Twentieth District of Texas. Gonzalez had served almost three decades when tapped to head the Banking Committee in 1988.

What made Gonzalez remarkable was his honesty and his literal view of the U.S. Constitution. If he detected the scent of a scandal, he followed his nose, even if it lead to dishonesty in his own party. Such an occurrence actually took place during the savings and loan scandal. He also once held unpublicized field hearings on living conditions in inner-city Los Angeles months before rioting broke out there in 1989. And he introduced impeachment proceedings against President George Bush, accusing him of buying votes at the United Nations and of blackmailing Congress.

A large man who always seems to wear an electric-blue suit and speak on CNN after the House had adjourned for the day, Gonzalez was a throwback. He is remembered by many for his lifelong commitment to justice and his service to the public.

the nation and gentler the face of the world," the president felt little of the kindness and gentleness for which he longed. Dana Carvey, a comedian on NBC-TV's "Saturday Night Live," perfected a savagely accurate characterization of Bush, and multimillionaire Texas businessman Ross Perot, an eventual presidential hopeful, sniped at the White House for failing to deal with the deficit and other matters.

Seeming perpetually ill at ease, George Bush would find his four years difficult and his popularity fluctuating more widely than many of his predecessors'. His wife, Barbara, with her mane of white hair, was popular and cordially received wherever she went. The mother of five grown children, her views were more moderate and expressed less forcefully than her husband's. An advocate of gun control, she also devoted herself to the promotion of literacy among young Americans, a project that was noncontroversial.

With Democrats slowly making gains in the last few elections, Republicans needed all the shaky ethics they

Barbara Bush speaking at a press conference for Child Abuse Prevention Month in 1988. Barbara Bush was a warm, outgoing woman who championed the rights of children, concentrating especially on childhood illiteracy. While many found fault with her husband, few criticized the first lady.

could find to maintain their congressional presence. Jim Wright of Texas, Speaker of the House of Representatives, was forced to resign in 1989 in connection with sixty-nine charges of ethics violations. He was soon followed by Representative Tony Coehlho of California, majority whip of the House. And while his 1989 Iran-contra conviction was overturned on appeal, Oliver North reminded America that George Bush knew more than he had admitted about the scandal.

Saving the Savings Accounts

Bush's first major, bipartisan move was to bail out the savings and loan business. The go-go eighties were gone-gone and with them the savings accounts of millions of Americans, many of them of modest means. They had put their faith and the money they could set aside in the local thrift institution, and the people who ran the institution had frittered it away on bad real estate investments. Not even a stock market that had surged since its frightful, five hundred-point drop in 1987 could help the S&Ls to recover. The savings and loan bailout was estimated to cost future taxpayers $400 billion over the next thirty years!

The president closed out the year by agreeing to increase the minimum hourly wage from the 1989 rate of $3.35 to $4.25 by 1991, with a training wage of $3.35 for sixteen-to-nineteen-year-olds in their first three months on the job. The $3.35 rate resulted in a forty-hour, pretax paycheck of $134 per week, or $7,468 per year. With unemployment at about 6 percent in 1989, fast-food businesses and other low-wage establishments found it difficult to attract help. Consequently, hourly wages of $5 or $6 were common. As the decade ended, more and more older Americans, many of them laid off from higher-paying jobs, were stuck filling orders, mopping floors, emptying trash, and closing up each night all across the country.

CHAPTER 11
The 1980s in Review

The United States took part in no major war in the 1980s. Communism was in decline all over Europe. The recession early in the decade was severe, but the recovery was heartening. The population grew older and more stable. Drug use declined. The Social Security system was rescued from financial oblivion. Space exploration rallied from disaster to pierce the heavens once again. Automakers opened the decade with inefficient, poorly built vehicles and closed it with a series of minivans, sedans, and pickup trucks that were fuel efficient and well assembled. The federal government pressed for deregulation, and business responded gratefully. With all this good news, why did so many Americans fear the future?

Two distinct visions, opposed on almost every subject, emerged more fully in the 1980s than ever before. The distinctions were sharp because, for the first time since the 1920s, true conservatives were in leadership roles and took advantage of their popularity to press for action on issues that for years had been out of the spotlight.

The Role of Government

America's legends are filled with gutsy frontierspeople who shrugged off the help of the cavalry to defend themselves as they pushed forward to the promised land. In the eighties, conservatives believed making people more self-sufficient would lower crime rates, cause welfare to dry up, give people a sense of purpose, and reinvigorate the entire country. Many wanted to pry the dependent off welfare — not to be mean but to teach them abruptly to stand on their own two feet. Those who opposed such abrupt action believed government could make a positive difference in people's lives. One problem with diminishing the role of government was that crooks could operate with

The space shuttle Discovery *is bathed in floodlights as it sits on the launch pad at Cape Canaveral on September 28, 1988. Its successful launch the next day marked America's return to piloted space flight after the* Challenger *disaster in 1986.*

almost total abandon. As an example, the failure of the federal Securities and Exchange Commission to be watchful played a part in the largest and most costly Wall Street fiasco in history, the 1987 insider stock-trading scandal (described in Chapter 4).

Religion and Politics

It has been said that religion is to Republicans as race is to Democrats. In other words, each party had a huge, ever-changing problem with which to deal. Big-business oriented, Republican conservatives manipulated religious Fundamentalists repeatedly in the 1980s, letting them expend their energy on matters of abortion, pornography, evolution, and prayer in schools in exchange for their votes. This coalition put Ronald Reagan in the White House twice and elected George Bush president next. But scandals among televangelists and outrageous pronouncements on the religious fringe led the more moderate Republicans to wonder about their new friends.

African-Americans and the Democrats

Because they were no longer in power, Democrats were let off the hook for much of the decade where race was concerned. African-Americans were overwhelmingly Democratic, yet the party continued to try their patience. Two eighties examples proved to be the 1984 and 1988 presidential campaigns of Jesse Jackson. Jackson emphasized equality for all and surrounded himself with people

Jesse Jackson, who was always popular with African-Americans, won over white voters in the 1984 and 1988 primaries. His campaign emphasized the need for economic justice, appealing to the growing number of unemployed in the nation.

representing every conceivable ethnic and racial group in his Rainbow Coalition. Yet establishment Democrats refused to hear his message, asking instead, "What does Jesse want?" African-American voters and progressive Democrats knew Jackson wanted a level playing field for all and to be taken seriously as a candidate. How long would African-Americans remain in the Democratic camp under such obtuse leadership?

Defense Expenditure Out of Hand

With an all-volunteer army and no conscription, it was easy for Americans to forget about defense. That proved costly, as contractors took advantage of the fears of conservative Republicans with cost overruns and ceaseless other ways to pry money out of the military. Already out of hand when the decade started, the federal budget deficit went absolutely crazy, paying for $1 billion aircraft, $10,000 toilets, and $1,000 hammers. Between defense and the exploration of space, the evening news regularly showed weapons and missiles misfiring, not firing at all, or exploding when least expected. Neither party had the courage to rein in the idiotic expenditures, despite the fact that like the Berlin Wall, European communism was crumbling and the threat of international war was diminishing.

Working Harder for Less Money

Prior to 1980, experts worried about what Americans might do with excessive amounts of leisure time.

That apprehension vanished between 1980 and 1990, as people worked more and more hours and had less discretionary time to themselves. There was a fear among all classes and ideologies that high-paying jobs were disappearing and low-paying jobs were the only kind available. Though unions fell out of favor, this was one message they got across repeatedly. The message was reinforced by the inability of fresh high school and college graduates to find meaningful work that was rewarding. Besides having less time, a family was more likely to have a grown son or daughter living at home for financial reasons during the eighties.

Doubts About Education

America has always been leery of intellectuals, and during the 1980s, the country became downright hostile to them. University professors were scorned for spending too much time in research and not enough time in class. Public-school teachers were warned that to strike for any reason could mean an end to their jobs. Ideologues conducted their own research, aiming at preconceived, incorrect notions such as the denial of the Holocaust. Ronald Reagan didn't help the teaching of science when he said he had trouble believing in evolution.

The Role of the Media

The media was more accessible than ever during the decade, but that did not make it better. On the contrary, television, radio, and print tried hard to deliver whatever they

> "And how stands the city on the winter night? More prosperous, more secure and happier than it was eight years ago. She's still a beacon .... for all who must have freedom."
>
> Ronald Reagan, in his farewell address, 1989

believed the public wanted. That became lurid, frequently incorrect tales about the rich and famous, confessions of all kinds, and poor imitations of investigative journalism. Carefully researched, probing journalism all but disappeared, resulting in scandals being quite mature by the time the media stumbled upon them. The only new method of investigation proved to be poring over data

aimed almost exclusively at them. Consequently, time spent in front of a television set increased. Americans' leisure time was bathed in the halo of a Sony, RCA, or Zenith, equipped with remote, which transported viewers from rock music to Rockefeller Center to a rocket launch and back. If the ability to communicate with the family deteriorated, television had to shoulder some of the blame. "Kill

West Berliners applaud as East Berliners drive through Checkpoint Charlie in the Berlin Wall after border restrictions are lifted in November 1989. In the late 1980s, the map of Europe was being redrawn, and the threat of war with the Communist bloc was vanishing.

bases, a method of which most professionals wanted no part. Trying hard to improve profits, news operations cut personnel, resulting in worse coverage.

A part of the media, television consolidated its power. Approximately 95 percent of U.S. homes had a television set, and half of those residences subscribed to a cable system. With dozens of channels to choose from, viewers quickly found stations

your television" bumper stickers were seen on vehicles belonging to people with a broader range of views.

Starstruck America

Entertainment was bigger business than ever before. Popular actors and actresses were aided by high-powered Hollywood publicity machines. The

Unemployed and homeless men sleep on a steam grate in front of the Department of the Interior Building in Washington, D.C., in 1982. Those without jobs and possessions received little comfort or support from the Reagan administration in the 1980s.

debut of a movie with a big star found that star on magazine covers, on morning-TV talk shows, on late-night talk shows, and in fifteen- and thirty-second advertising spots. The number of actors and actresses who were stars for a matter of weeks was startling. Equally startling, following the initial wave of publicity, was the tabloid journalism that trailed these usually beautiful and briefly famous people. Americans knew better than to idolize an actress or a football player, but they did it anyway, again and again.

Morality and Medicine

Deep, troubling questions arose over when life begins, how long it exists, and when it ends. Individuals with terminal illnesses could be kept alive for weeks with space-age equipment. Fed through tubes and forced to breath by machines, these unfortunate people no longer in control of anything forced their next of kin into making decisions about letting them die in peace. Physicians, seen as one source of soaring health costs, also were viewed as the bearers of immense egos. Many were willing to operate on the most elderly or sickly patient in the conceited belief that any life could and should be prolonged and that they were the ones to do it.

A Lack of Support for the Arts

The arts shrank, in part because politicians and others wondered if any work needing tax money to survive was worth saving. The National Endowment for the Arts came under fire for giving money to artists who produced left-wing or antireligious works in questionable taste. Grassroots art flourished in many parts of the country, but for every genuine exhibit, portrayal, reading, performance, or creation there were dozens of cheesy art fairs and slipshod performances of aging Broadway hits. The 1980s might be remembered for distinctive architecture, but not for the originality or quality of the other art produced. In keeping with the decade's big theme of greed, the best-remembered art was that which fetched the highest price.

New Technology Means Better Products

Technology took several paths. Like art, much of the most technologically advanced breakthroughs were also the most expensive. Technology on the factory floor became a commitment to quality — subcontractors were expected to deliver parts so perfect they would not have to be inspected before being used in the product being assembled. Zero-defects products poured out of American industry with increasing frequency, led by companies such as Compaq, General Electric, and Motorola. Technology also gained speed, as companies at widely different sites on the globe raced to get similar products into the marketplace first. Product quality, taken for granted by many consumers, made immense strides.

The Changing Role of Women

Many people assumed that a woman working outside the home would receive cooperation from her family. They were wrong, as survey after survey indicated that women with outside jobs — and the vast majority of women did go off to work — remained the ones who cooked the meals, made the beds, cleaned the bathroom, and did the shopping. Neither men nor women had time to spare, but women were forced to make time to keep the household in one piece. Perhaps because women knew this, they were marrying a bit later and waiting to have children. Much as they may have wanted kids, rearing a child would fall disproportionately to them.

Asian Arrivals Cause Resentment

Unobtrusively, Koreans, East Indians, Southeast Asians, and people from all areas of the Middle East became more numerous and more evident in the eighties. Foreigners, armed with their life savings, came to the U.S. and often purchased businesses, which they found to be quite reasonable due to the relative decline of the dollar's value. This created resentment among Hispanics, but even more among

strange or extreme religions, bizarre politics, an avalanche of faddish consumer products, a wave of entertainment offerings, and a barrage of frequently contradictory statistics, it managed to at least tread water. The divorce rate leveled off, though prison populations continued to climb.

A cloud of pollution hangs over the city of Denver in 1983. The natural environment suffered as a result of the Reagan administration's hostility to antipollution measures.

African-Americans, who witnessed the almost instant success of people who knew little English and even less about the country. Success in school by sons and daughters of these new arrivals made some black parents wonder if the immigrant children were receiving favored treatment.

Family Matters

Attacked from all sides, the family nevertheless survived in the 1980s. Threatened by unemployment,

There were more "random acts of kindness" and random shootings in households. And, while privacy was threatened as never before, the average family found once-luxurious items such as air travel and cruise vacations more accessible than ever.

The Twenties and the Eighties

The 1980s have been compared to the 1920s primarily because both decades experienced pro-business,

The Live Aid concert in Philadelphia's JFK Stadium in July 1985. Live Aid was initiated by Irish singer Bob Geldof to raise money for famine relief in Ethiopia. He organized all-star rock concerts in America and Britain. They were broadcast to over 150 countries, and millions of people pledged money.

Republican rule. At the end of either ten-year period, it was remarkable how little of what happened in Washington affected the average American. He or she was much more likely to be pleased that a street was paved or dismayed that the snowplow skipped a block than whether a defense appropriation was passed or a tax bill transformed into law. Americans in the eighties frequently felt that whatever took place in Washington had little or no direct bearing on their lives.

KEY DATES

1980

April 24 — Eight Americans die and five are injured in an ill-fated attempt to rescue hostages held in the U.S. embassy in Tehran, Iran.

May 18 — Mount Saint Helens explodes in the State of Washington with a force five hundred times that of the atomic bomb dropped on Hiroshima.

November 4 — Ronald Reagan becomes the fortieth president of the United States in a landslide victory over incumbent Jimmy Carter.

1981

January 20 — The fifty-two Americans being held by Iran are released minutes after Ronald Reagan is sworn in.

March 30 — President Reagan is shot and gravely wounded in Washington, D.C., by a young gunman, John Hinckley, later found to be insane.

April 12 — The space shuttle *Columbia* lifts off on its first flight and returns safely two days later.

September 21 — The first female U.S. Supreme Court justice, Sandra Day O'Connor, is approved by the Senate, ninety-nine to zero.

1982

July — The Equal Rights Amendment, which would have outlawed certain kinds of discrimination against women, is defeated after a ten-year fight for ratification.

November 5 — The highest unemployment rate since 1940, a total of 10.4 percent, is reported.

1983

June 18 — Sally Ride becomes America's first female astronaut when the space shuttle *Challenger* is launched.

October 23 — A total of 241 U.S. Marines and sailors die in a terrorist suicide bombing in Beirut, Lebanon.

October 25 — U.S. forces join Caribbean nations in invading Grenada, where elected officials had been overthrown and Cuban military advisors had been running the country.

1984

March — Separate Constitutional amendments that would have permitted prayer in public schools are rejected by the Senate.

May 7 — Seven chemical companies reach an out-of-court settlement in a suit filed on behalf of hundreds of Vietnam War veterans who believed they had been poisoned by a defoliant known as Agent Orange.

November 6 — In a forty-nine-state landslide victory, the Reagan-Bush team beats Mondale-Ferraro in the presidential election.

1985

July 13 — Philadelphia and London are sites for Live Aid, a fundraising rock concert that results in $70 million for starving people in Africa.

November 19-20 — President Reagan and Mikhail Gorbachev, the Soviet general secretary, hold a summit and talk privately for five hours in the city of Geneva, Switzerland.

1986

January 20 — The United States has a new national holiday, Martin Luther King Jr. Day.

January 28 — The space shuttle *Challenger* explodes just moments after liftoff, killing six astronauts and a civilian teacher, Christa McAuliffe. NASA is later found negligent.

April 15 — U.S. jets attack targets in Libya in retaliation for the bombing by Libyan-backed terrorists of a West Berlin disco blown up nine days earlier.

November — The public learns that the U.S. has sent spare parts and ammunition to Iran.

November 14 — Ivan Boesky is fined $100 million and will serve a prison sentence for illegal insider trading.

1987

February 27 — A federal commission finds President Reagan confused and uninformed on the Iran-contra affair.

May–August — Iran-contra hearings are held before House and Senate committees. President Reagan continues to deny knowledge, while Lieutenant Colonel Oliver North, a minor White House aide, is saddled with much of the blame for the illegal project.

October 19 — The Dow Jones Industrial Average plunges 508 points after hitting a record high of 2,722 in August.

December 8 — President Reagan and Soviet leader Mikhail Gorbachev agree on additional dismantling of missiles.

1988

February 4 — Grand juries in Florida indict General Manuel Noriega, the dictator of Panama, charging that he aided Colombian drug lords.

May 4 — Nearly 1.4 million aliens living in the U.S. seek amnesty under a new federal immigration policy. Half live in California, and more than two-thirds of the national total entered the country from Mexico.

May 31 — President Reagan visits Moscow and assails the Soviet human rights record.

November 8 — George Bush is elected the forty-first U.S. president. Bush and Vice President Dan Quayle capture 54 percent of the vote versus 46 percent for Michael Dukakis and Lloyd Bentsen.

1989

March 24 — The largest oil spill in U.S. history takes place when the *Exxon Valdez* strikes a reef in Prince William Sound, Alaska.

May 4 — Oliver North is convicted of several charges related to the Iran-contra scandal. The conviction eventually will be overturned.

August 9 — Legislation is passed to bail out the troubled savings and loan industry, but at a cost of $166 billion over ten years and $400 billion over thirty years.

October 17 — An earthquake centered in northern California is seen on national television because a World Series game was scheduled to be played in San Francisco at the time of the quake.

December 20 — U.S. troops invade Panama, overthrowing Manuel Noriega, who surrenders January 3, 1990, after hiding in the Vatican's embassy.

FOR FURTHER RESEARCH

Bredeson, Carmen. *The Challenger Disaster: Tragic Space Flight (American Disasters).* Springfield, NJ: Enslow, 1999.

Chafe, William H. *The Road to Equality: Women Since 1962 (Young Oxford History of Women in the United States, Vol 10).* New York: Oxford University Press, 1998.

Dils, Tracey E. *The Exxon Valdez (Great Disasters: Reforms and Ramifications).* Broomall, PA: Chelsea House, 1998.

Epstein, Dan. *The 80's: 20th Century Pop Culture.* Broomall, CT: Chelsea House, 2000.

Feinstein, Stephen. *The 1980s: From Ronald Reagan to Mtv (Decades of the Twentieth Century).* Springfield, NJ: Enslow, 2000.

Gilbert, Adrian. *The 80s.* Austin, TX: Steck Vaughn, 2000.

Kallen, Stuart. *The 1980s (Cultural History of the United States Through the Decades).* San Diego, CA: Lucent Books, 1999.

Kern, Montague. *Thirty-Second Politics: Political Advertising in the Eighties.* Westport, CT: Greenwood, 1991.

Sewall, George T. Editor. *The Eighties: A Reader.* Cambridge, MA: Perseus Book Group, 1998.

Sherrow Victoria. *San Francisco Earthquake, 1989: Death and Destruction (American Disasters).* Springfield, NJ: Enslow, 1998.

Time-Life Editors. *Pride and Prosperity: The 80s (Our American Century).* New York: Time-Life Books, 1999.

Movies
The Empire Strikes Back, LucasFilm, 1980.

Raging Bull, United Artists/Chorloff-Winkler Productions, 1980.

Raiders of the Lost Ark, LucasFilm/Paramount, 1981.

Blade Runner, Blade Runner Partnership/The Ladd Company, 1982.

E.T. - The Extra-Terrestrial, Universal Pictures, 1982.

Amadeus, Orion, 1984.

Contemporary Music
All Night Long, Lionel Richie, 1980.

Billie Jean, Michael Jackson, 1983.

Born in the USA, Bruce Springsteen, 1984.

Material Girl, Madonna, 1985.

Contemporary Literature
Cosmos, Carl Sagan, 1980.

The Color Purple, Alice Walker, 1982.

It, Stephen King, 1986.

Beloved, Toni Morrison, 1987.

And the Band Played On: Politics, People, and the AIDS Epidemic, Randy Shilts, 1987.

Television Shows
1980 *Dallas*
1981 *Hill Street Blues*
1982 *Cheers*
1984 *The Cosby Show*
1986 The Challenger explosion
1986 *Oprah Winfrey Show*
1987 *Eyes on the Prize*
1988 *America's Most Wanted*
1989 The San Francisco Earthquake

Websites
Culture, politics in the 1980s
http://eightiesclub.tripod.com

Lots of links to topics of the 80s
http://dir.yahoo.com/Arts/Humanities/History/By_Time_Period/20th_Century/1980s/Popular_Culture

INDEX

Page numbers in *italic* indicate picture; page numbers in **bold** indicate biography

Page numbers in *italic* indicate picture; page numbers in **bold** indicate biography

Page numbers in *italic* indicate picture; page numbers in **bold** indicate biography

ACKNOWLEDGMENTS

The author and publishers wish to thank the following for permission to reproduce copyright material:

Aquarius Library: 1224; The Bettmann Archive: 1169, 1193; Peter Newark's American Pictures: 1254; Reuters/Bettmann: *frontispiece*, 1178, 1179, 1189, 1195, 1197, 1210, 1212, 1213, 1215, 1217, 1219, 1221, 1227, 1232, 1234, 1238, 1239, 1249, 1262, 1274; Reuters/Bettman Newsphotos: 1183, 1187, 1190, 1194, 1214, 1223, 1233, 1235, 1242, 1285; Science Photo Library: 1248, 1253, 1257; UPI/Bettmann: 1159, 1160, 1161, 1162, 1163, 1165, 1166, 1168, 1171, 1172, 1173, 1174, 1177, 1180, 1181, 1182, 1185, 1186, 1188, 1191, 1200, 1203, 1205, 1206, 1207, 1216, 1218, 1220, 1225, 1228, 1229, 1230, 1240, 1243, 1244, 1246, 1247, 1252, 1256, 1258, 1259, 1263, 1266, 1267, 1269, 1271, 1273, 1278, 1281, 1282, 1288; UPI/Bettmann Newsphotos: 1174, 1198, 1199, 1202, 1212, 1245, 1251, 1260, 1265, 1270, 1275, 1276, 1280, 1283, 1286, 1289.

The illustrations on pages 1176, 1209, 1261, and 1277 are by Rafi Mohammed.

Page numbers in *italic* indicate picture; page numbers in **bold** indicate biography